Composition and the Academy

A Study of Writing Program Administration

Carol P. Hartzog

The Modern Language Association of America
New York   1986

Copyright © 1986 by The Modern Language Association of America

Library of Congress Cataloging-in-Publication Data

Hartzog, Carol P., 1940–
  Composition and the academy.

  Bibliography: p.
  1. English language—Rhetoric—Study and teaching—
United States.   2. Writing centers—United States—
Administration.   3. Interdisciplinary approach in
education.   I. Title.
PE1405.U6H37   1986   808'.042'071273   86-16278
ISBN 0-87352-377-6
ISBN 0-87352-378-4 (pbk.)

Published by The Modern Language Association of America
10 Astor Place, New York, New York 10003

For
Sarah, Steve, and Jon

Contents

Tables

In the text, survey questions serve as table headings whenever possible. In this listing, brief descriptive titles identify the tables.

Preface

Knowledge is to be found not only in demonstrations, it can also be found in fiction, reflexion, narrative accounts, institutional regulations, and political decisions.

Michel Foucault, *The Archaeology of Knowledge*

AT ISSUE TODAY IS composition's relation to English studies, a relation that poses administrative as well as intellectual problems. Though writing programs need some kind of departmental base, they serve an interdisciplinary purpose. Should composition be viewed as an independent scholarly discipline? Should writing programs continue to be housed in English departments? The decisions being made on individual campuses—often on an ad hoc basis—both influence and reflect attitudes toward composition. Further, the entire effort to find an appropriate place for composition within the university raises questions about traditional departmental structures and their effect on liberal education. As a result, we need to understand how writing programs are now being administered on campuses across the country.

I offer here a report on writing programs at institutions belonging to the Association of American Universities (AAU). It includes not just statistics and my analysis of them but also narrative accounts, perhaps with some element of fiction in the telling or retelling, and a good deal of comment on political struggles, tactics, and decisions. To understand the place that composition holds in the academy today, we must go beyond its theory, research, and pedagogy to program administration, and to understand that administration, we need to listen to the wisdom of its strategists.

My report on writing programs is based on questionnaires mailed to 52 AAU campuses and returned by 44 program directors or department chairs, on in-person or telephone interviews with 35 respondents, and finally on three campus visits. In all, I received information from 41 (or 79%) of the AAU campuses. The first section of the questionnaire contained twenty-four questions on program administration; the second, sixteen questions addressed specifically to the program director. In interviews, I asked supplementary questions about the programs and their histories, as well as about composition and its status on campus. During the campus visits, in meetings with administrators, directors, and teachers, I asked how and how well the programs worked and how they fit within university structures.

This study can be seen as a complement to earlier studies of writing programs. I would mention in particular a study of writing program assessment

funded by the Fund for Postsecondary Education and the University of
Texas and detailed in a series of technical reports. The second report,
released in 1981, presents descriptive statistics on 127 college and university
writing programs (Witte et al. 3). Its authors—Stephen P. Witte, Paul R.
Meyer, Thomas P. Miller, and Lester Faigley—observed at the time, "our
national projections should be viewed with some caution. . . . Nevertheless,
we believe our projections give the best (if not the only) estimate to date of
how writing programs work across the country"(10).

My study can also be seen as a complement to works describing individual
programs and departments, like the MLA's publications in the Options for
the Teaching of English series (see Cowan; Neel). It supplements recent articles on writing across the curriculum and on program administration.
Finally, it relates to works like *Composition and Literature: Bridging the
Gap*, edited by Winifred Bryan Horner; *The Rhetorical Tradition and Modern Writing*, edited by James J. Murphy; and *Textual Power: Literary
Theory and the Teaching of English*, by Robert Scholes—works drawing
connections between theory and classroom practice and among composition,
rhetoric, and literature.

Having said something about what this study is, let me also explain what
it is not. It is not, nor does it pretend to be, a comprehensive study of writing
programs in the country today. I have selected AAU programs not because
they are truly representative of all programs, including those at two- and
four-year colleges. Obviously, they are not. I have selected AAU programs
for several reasons. First, they exist on a clearly defined and limited set of
campuses, those of major research universities that have been invited into
the membership of the AAU. These campuses are all of a kind, and yet,
within that kind, they vary tremendously: public, private, independent;
land-grant, technical, and Ivy League, with enrollments ranging from 1,700
to 64,000. Second, many of these programs have already gained visibility,
often because of the quality of their leadership. Many writing program
directors on AAU campuses are influencing composition studies, and their
programs have also become well known. We have not, however, always
known about their programs in detail. Third, questions about the status and
identity of composition have to do not only with teaching but also with
research. Is it possible to do substantial work in this field—and earn
traditional academic rewards for that work? For at least one answer to this
question, we need to look to research universities, institutions valuing and
advancing research. If I have a fourth reason, it's that I know one such institution well and thus have experience that may help me understand and
interpret the results of this study.

My aim here is not to show these programs in array or disarray but, rather,
to understand the place of composition in the academy. How do programs
and their directors address and perhaps solve some of the major problems in
composition today? Where does composition belong, intellectually and administratively, on the campuses of major research universities? My report, I
hope, will reveal some of the struggles, the issues, and the politics in these

programs and also describe the fit between the programs and their institutions.

I recognize the limits of this project. While my sample population includes many programs with unusual resources, leadership, and support, others are missing—even some within the AAU—that deserve careful study. The writing program at Texas, Austin, has earned national attention, first because of its leadership and sophistication, then because of its fate. Yet that program did not participate in my study, perhaps because of the turmoil it was going through during 1984-85. A story of dramatic reversal, not mine to tell, appeared in the *Chronicle of Higher Education* (see Hairston; Heller). The absence of this program, unfortunate and symbolic, affects the tenor of my report.

A second note of caution comes from one of the respondents: not all campuses have advanced as far and as quickly as others in developing programs that integrate current theory and research into classroom instruction. "Most universities, I suspect, are like this one," he told me in describing a state university only now beginning to question the traditional split between freshman writing and the rest of the English department, only now discovering what an enterprise composition has become and how assertive its advocates are. There changes are gradually being made, given external pressures and some alleviation of budget restrictions. With resources, needs, and interests differing substantially from campus to campus, the solutions tried on any one campus may not serve on others. Instead, the dynamics—the strategies tried in these institutions—hold central importance. As a result, I have set out to examine strategies rather than to develop models that can be followed, and my findings may lead toward understanding rather than toward easy application.

For studying entities as complex as writing programs, a written survey, I know, has limits. One respondent wrote:

> As I am sure is the case at a lot of institutions, particularly large ones, our curriculum in composition has a unique and tangled history that makes it difficult to understand and in some ways to modify. We have, for example, different requirements in each of the undergraduate colleges, so that Arts and Sciences requires 2 semesters, some specify one particular freshman course, and others have no requirement at all. We have 1,400 students in one course called Composition, which many colleges specify, not necessarily with our advice, because of its captivating title. The course is taught by every kind of faculty, from full professor to new graduate student, with a minimum of supervision. Seems like madness, but it has its history and even its virtues. But what it doesn't do is fit surveys very well.

The written survey gave me some statistical information on the programs and their directors. But because, indeed, programs do not fit surveys very well, I added the option of supplementary telephone or in-person interviews. My particular interests led me to conduct interviews rather than to read program descriptions, syllabi, or student essays. I wanted to learn about the mechanisms and design of writing programs and about attitudes toward composition. To do so, I needed to talk with those in charge more than to see the products of their work. Another study, much more extensive, could indeed add other dimensions of research. For my investigation, however, I valued most the chance to ask directors questions about program administration and about the climate for their work. From these interviews, I began to see how programs have taken their present forms and to understand some of the forces and relations involved. I also came to know and respect my colleagues who are directing the programs—and directing them with care and imagination. Finally, I visited three campuses—North Carolina, Chapel Hill; the University of Pennsylvania; and Harvard—to study their writing programs in more detail. In doing so, I again focused more on management than on individual classrooms. While I came away with some insight into the administrative structures and strategies being used—effectively—on these campuses, much more remains to be learned about each program.

As this report shows, my interest in administration is matched by my conviction that the current debates about composition have implications reaching far beyond placement procedures and writing requirements. If those now designing writing programs want the conditions that best enable their students and faculty members to work productively together, they also want much more. They want programs that fit into the intellectual and administrative structures of the academy. As much as an academic unit needs some way of operating effectively, it also needs a certain disciplinary stature. Yet writing programs can be many things in themselves, and the field they represent can be variously defined. We are now seeing a field in transition: writing programs are struggling not just for security but for dignity. While these programs need coherence and strength—internal characteristics—to ensure their viability, they also need close relations with other academic programs and departments. These relations can be curricular, resulting from the connection between writing and various disciplines across campus or, more traditionally, between writing and English studies. They can also be administrative, created through adjunct courses or through advisory committees, faculty appointments, and lines of reporting. These connections, however, do not fully explain why debates about composition can have implications for faculty members in other fields.

The larger importance of these debates lies in the questions they raise about normal academic structures and procedures. Does it matter whether or not composition is a discipline? How can we know whether it is or not? And who should decide just what it ought to be? At issue here is the relation between an academic discipline and its departmental manifestations on individual campuses.

Behind my work lie several assumptions. A discipline is not simply a body of knowledge but an approach, a system of thought, an academic structure—intellectual and administrative. To understand an emerging discipline, we need to consider how that discipline is made concrete in the institutional setting, how it is set up, what people say for and against it. At a time of much uncertainty about composition as a field of study, it is appropriate to consider how writing programs have been established and how they work and, more broadly, to see how they help universities meet their educational initiatives and goals. Such a study can show something of how a discipline is defined, how it comes into being.

The questions now being asked about composition, Janice M. Lauer has noted, "are normal and appropriate for a developing field, which must define itself" (20). We can learn from a discipline trying to mark off its boundaries, to develop a system of thought. But we must expect to find radical impurity: the discipline will never be defined simply on the basis of its theory and research; it will be determined as well by the academic politics that govern it. We need, therefore, to be especially sensitive to language—the language used in conversations and debates about the programs. To that end, I have tried throughout this report to incorporate the language used by the directors and chairs in charge of these programs.

Because this is a time of questioning and change, we should closely watch the political debates about where writing programs should be housed. The justifications offered, the struggles, the conceptual disagreements are instructive, as are the opinions expressed on composition. Because some feel that composition shouldn't be identified as an academic discipline, we need a sense of what is evolving. How is composition, in flux, becoming (or failing to become) a discipline? The issue is both conceptual and political. A discipline may not be contained within a single department. Yet, given ordinary university structures, a discipline needs some departmental base and some recognizable academic identity. Those who are now talking about discourse studies or cultural studies are trying to change the territory for discussion. We see in composition, then, both an impulse toward a place of its own and an impulse toward dispersion.

From my study of AAU writing programs, I've learned how variously they are addressing both the conceptual and the administrative problems before them. As Stephen Witte and his colleagues reported, "if there is to be drawn a major conclusion from our examination of the writing programs we surveyed, it is that they are generally very different from one another, that they are each designed to address primarily the local needs of the institution, the department, and the student body" (120). As I look at the variety of programs before me, I think of Stanley Fish considering whether "there are (at least potentially) as many experiences as there are readers" (4). Yet in my study I have seen patterns forming—structural, historical patterns revealed through practices, attitudes, conflicts, and decisions. I've observed the kinds of changes that are being made, and I've listened to explanations of success and failure. From these explanations, we all can learn.

Acknowledgments

At every stage of this project, I have depended on my colleagues for help, encouragement, and advice. The idea itself originated in conversations with Willis G. Regier and Robert E. Bjork, and to them I am deeply grateful. The survey took shape as Eve Fielder and Mike Rose explained how it might best be designed, and various drafts were improved by suggestions from Phyllis P. Franklin, Lynn Z. Bloom, Winifred Bryan Horner, and Elaine P. Maimon. During the weeks spent in developing, preparing, mailing, and then tabulating the survey, it belonged to Susan Bukowski, Lourdes Everett, and Antonio Serrata as much as to me. Every record, draft, and table seemed to need Michael E. Cohen's expert advice on word processing. While I was involved in this study, I relied on the steady support of the UCLA Writing Programs faculty and staff, who taught me what a writing program can be. To Lauren Cammack, my assistant for five years, I am indebted not only for her talent in academic management but also for her friendship and warm good humor.

I want especially to acknowledge those who have given me the information and insight needed for this report. The program directors and department chairs named in the list of respondents have been overwhelmingly helpful and gracious in explaining how their programs are designed. Erika Lindemann, Richard Marius, Peshe Kuriloff, and David Espey—together with administrators, faculty members, teaching assistants, and staff on their campuses—welcomed me and let me watch their programs in action. I value their kindness to me as a guest and their openness to each of my questions.

My special thanks also to those who have encouraged me in this project or read drafts of the report. All the directors and chairs who were interviewed carefully reviewed my comments on their programs. A number of people checked the accuracy of the case studies and concluding remarks on the programs I visited. For this important help, I thank not only Erika Lindemann, Richard Marius, Peshe Kuriloff, and David Espey but also Robert Bain, Stephen S. Birdsall, Lowry Pei, Donald Stone, Joel Conarroe, Thomas Ehrlich, Robert Lucid, and Elaine P. Maimon. Mike Rose read part 1, asking the right questions and offering extremely useful advice on the tables. Richard A. Lanham read the conclusion and offered me needed reassurance. Lynn Z. Bloom helped me see the bibliography as a text to be revised, and Richard L. Larson assisted me with that revision. For patiently reading the entire manuscript and offering me their wisdom and encouragement, I thank William D. Schaefer, Linda Morris, Anne Ruggles Gere, Ben W. McClelland, and—when I needed perspective and guidance for final revisions—Linda H. Peterson. Together, they helped me see what needed fixing in the manuscript; even more important, they encouraged me to say what remained unsaid.

I am happily indebted to those who have helped bring this work to publication: Phyllis P. Franklin encouraged me to carry out my study and present its results to the MLA. Carl R. Lovitt asked incisive questions about the preliminary report, making my work on the final manuscript easier. Walter S. Achtert offered firm editorial support from the time when I first wrote him about this project. And Claire Kehrwald Cook, because of her talent in copyediting, gave me new respect for the text that we have now worked on together. As I completed my work on the manuscript, Barbara Brandon assisted me with correspondence and mailings. When I received the galleys, Patricia Chittenden helped me proofread them. For her skill in handling the book's production, I am grateful to Judith Altreuter.

Others deserve acknowledgment as well: Shari Zimmerman and Janis Forman shared in the frustration and joy of my writing. And Tallman Trask III helped me believe I could finish this book. In a special category are my three children, Sarah, Steve, and Jon: they kept me centered and helped me work throughout this project.

Because a great many people have influenced this report, whatever value it has reflects their understanding, example, cooperation, and advice. Its faults I accept as my own.

I have received financial support not only from UCLA Writing Programs but from two other sources: the Council of Writing Program Administrators awarded me a grant that helped cover the initial expenses of the survey and the telephone interviews, and UCLA's executive vice chancellor, William D. Schaefer, appointed me special assistant to the chancellor for spring quarter 1985, generously allowing me the time and the resources I needed for making campus visits and for completing this study. I am indebted to all who have helped finance my work.

Please note that some sections of this report appeared in an earlier form in "Composition and the Academy: A Preliminary Report on AAU Writing Programs," presented at the 1984 MLA convention and published in the *ADE Bulletin*.

The Sample

Respondents

The titles listed here for respondents are those reported in 1984-85. Since then several respondents have taken new positions, on these or other campuses.

Brown University: DeWitt Allen, Director of Composition, Department of English
University of California, Berkeley: Kim Davis, Coordinator, Subject A
University of California, Los Angeles: Carol P. Hartzog, Director, UCLA Writing Programs; Mike Rose, Director of Freshman Writing, UCLA Writing Programs

University of California, San Diego: Charles Cooper, Coordinator, Third College Writing Program; Coordinator, Campus Writing Programs

California Institute of Technology: J. Kent Clark, Professor, Department of Literature

Carnegie-Mellon University: Gary F. Waller, Head, Department of English

Case Western Reserve University: William R. Siebenschuh, Director of Composition and the Writing Center, Department of English

Catholic University of America: Jean D. Moss, Director of Rhetoric and Composition, Department of English

University of Chicago: Joseph Williams, Professor, Department of English

Clark University: Leone C. Scanlon, Director, Writing Center

University of Colorado, Boulder: Thomas Lyons, Director, College Expository Writing Program

Duke University: Carl L. Anderson, Professor, Department of English

Harvard University: Richard Marius, Director, Expository Writing Program

University of Illinois, Urbana: Robert L. Schneider, Director of Freshman Rhetoric, Department of English

Indiana University, Bloomington: Marilyn S. Sternglass, Director of First Year Studies, Department of English

University of Iowa: Richard Lloyd-Jones, Chair, Department of English

Iowa State University: Richard J. Zbaracki, Professor, Department of English

University of Kansas: Haskell Springer, Director, Freshman-Sophomore English, Department of English

University of Maryland, College Park: Eugene Hammond, Associate Professor, Department of English

Massachusetts Institute of Technology: James Paradis, Head, Writing Program

McGill University: Robert Lecker, Associate Chair, Department of English

University of Michigan: William Ingram, Director, Program in Composition, Department of English; Jay L. Robinson, Chair, English Composition Board

Michigan State University: Jay B. Ludwig, Director of Composition, Department of English; Henry Silverman, Chairperson, Department of American Thought and Language

University of Minnesota, Minneapolis: Donald Ross, Director, Program in Composition and Communication; St. Paul: Thomas Pearsall, Head, Department of Rhetoric

University of Missouri, Columbia: Winifred Bryan Horner, Professor, Department of English

University of Nebraska, Lincoln: Gerry Brookes, Coordinator of Composition Courses, Department of English; F. M. Link, Chair, Department of English

University of North Carolina, Chapel Hill: Erika Lindemann, Director of Composition, Department of English

University of Oregon: John T. Gage, Director of Composition, Department of English

University of Pennsylvania: Peshe Kuriloff, Coordinator, Writing Center and Writing across the University, Department of English

University of Pittsburgh: David Bartholomae, Director of Composition, Department of English

Princeton University: Michael Robertson, Director, Literature 151, Department of English

Purdue University: Leonora Woodman, Director of Freshman Composition, Department of English

University of Rochester: J. W. Johnson, Professor, Department of English

University of Southern California: Betty Bamberg, Director, Freshman Writing
    Program
Stanford University: Charles Fifer, Director of Freshman English, Department of
    English
Tulane University: Les Perelman, Director of Freshman English, Department of
    English
Vanderbilt University: Scott Colley, Associate Dean, College of Arts and Science;
    Jenny Snyder, Director of Freshman English, Department of English
University of Virginia: Charlene M. Sedgwick, Director of Writing Programs, De-
    partment of English
Washington University: Robert Wiltenburg, Director of Freshman Composition,
    Department of English
University of Wisconsin, Madison: Martin Nystrand, Associate Professor, De-
    partment of English
Yale University: Linda H. Peterson, Director of Expository Writing

Respondents Interviewed

By telephone only

Allen (Brown)
Bartholomae (Pittsburgh)
Brookes (Nebraska, Lincoln)
Colley (Vanderbilt)
Davis (Berkeley)
Fifer (Stanford)
Ingram (Michigan)
Lecker (McGill)
Lloyd-Jones (Iowa)
Ludwig (Michigan State)
Lyons (Colorado, Boulder)
Moss (Catholic)

Pearsall (Minnesota, St. Paul)
Perelman (Tulane)
Peterson (Yale)
Robertson (Princeton)
Ross (Minnesota, Minneapolis)
Scanlon (Clark)
Schneider (Illinois, Urbana)
Sedgwick (Virginia)
Silverman (Michigan State)
Waller (Carnegie-Mellon)
Wiltenburg (Washington)
Zbaracki (Iowa State)

In person only

Bamberg (USC)
Gage (Oregon)
Marius (Harvard)
Rose (UCLA)
Woodman (Purdue)

By telephone and in person

Hammond (Maryland, College
    Park)
Kuriloff (Penn)
Lindemann (North Carolina,
    Chapel Hill)
Robinson (Michigan)
Sternglass (Indiana, Bloo-
    mington)
Williams (Chicago)

Statistics on Response

Number of campuses represented: 41.   Of the 52 campuses belonging to the Association of American Universities at the time of the survey, 79% responded. (Note that the campuses at Minneapolis and St. Paul are treated as one campus of the University of Minnesota.)

Number of respondents: 47.   All respondents except Lecker, Lloyd-Jones, and Rose returned survey questionnaires. Lecker phoned to explain that McGill does not offer writing courses; Lloyd-Jones responded to survey and interview questions by phone; Rose responded in person to interview questions about his views of composition and the status of the program.

Number of programs represented: 44.   Three more programs than campuses are represented because four campuses each have two writing programs and one campus has none. There are three fewer programs than respondents for these reasons: (1) Because McGill does not have a writing program, I counted McGill only in tallying responses to the question, "Does one academic unit coordinate all writing instruction on your campus?" (2) Though both Link and Brookes at Nebraska, Lincoln, returned the written survey, Brookes completed only the questions addressed to the program director. In making my tallies, I entered Brookes's responses to these questions and Link's responses to questions about program administration. (3) For UCLA, I completed the written survey, and Rose responded to interview questions.

Number of responses possible on most questions: 44.   Although the tabulations of responses usually indicate one for each program represented, on some questions respondents checked each applicable item, so that the number of responses is greater than 44. When fewer than 44 replied to a question, the total number of responses is noted.

PART ONE

A Survey of Writing Programs

CHAPTER 1

Profiles of Change

M Y STUDY OF AAU WRITING PROGRAMS focuses primarily on the academic year 1984-85, the year in which I conducted the written survey, interviews, and campus visits. While the study shows how those programs were structured and administered during that year, it also suggests how they took shape and what plans they have for development. Seen in the context of the ten years preceding the study, these programs are characterized by dramatic change. Though academic structures, procedures, and policies develop over a long period, most respondents can identify a certain year or range of years as a time of major change within their programs. This fact of change deserves attention both because it clarifies our understanding of the programs as they existed during a particular year and because it coincides with a larger pattern of change within the field of composition.

While writing programs keep adjusting their fit within their own institutions, they also change to reflect developments in the field. They absorb and influence what is currently understood about writing even as they expand, cut back, or change their services. If the ideal writing program would serve students—all students—well, involve and satisfy faculty members, and hold a place of respect on campus (reflected in the university's table of organization as in its budget), then some programs, of course, come closer than others to the ideal. But even more intriguing than the details of this ideal is the act of imagining and trying to achieve it. As a result, I have aimed not so much to find a single prototype as to watch programs in the process of change.

To learn the histories of the writing programs I was studying, I asked several survey questions about programmatic and budgetary changes and then, in interviews, invited directors to tell their programs' stories. What follows is a brief composite of their remarks. During the sixties, departments gave up freshman English or at least stopped requiring it. Writing programs—or collections of writing courses—suffered neglect, as well as disrespect. Reportedly on a book salesman's recommendation, one department discontinued its placement procedures and reduced its freshman courses from five to two, expecting (accurately) that fewer students would fail. At the same time, courses proliferated on many campuses. One director described his department's offerings as a cafeteria curriculum. The fates of other programs? "For a while you couldn't give the program away." "Our program was run by graduate students from 1969 to 1973." "Before I was hired to run the program, it was directed by someone who did this as an avocation." "Ten years ago, there was no program."

By the midseventies, universities were again feeling pressures for change. Faculties were beginning to realize that their students did have problems with writing, students were demanding writing courses, and the faculty members and administrators who had been interested in writing gained support. In addition, the poor quality of students' writing was receiving public attention. Given the new concern about writing, universities responded. Many reinstituted a writing requirement; some added or strengthened their offerings in technical and business writing; some, wanting to reassert composition as a humanistic discipline, began building up faculties and programs in rhetoric and composition. Remedial writing courses changed from grammar courses to writing courses. At the same time, job competition increased, and prospective faculty members faced new realities in the profession. Financial problems and the resulting cutbacks in hiring meant that fewer jobs were available in literature, and with increasing emphasis on writing, the new PhDs who found academic positions could expect to teach composition.

After what is described as a time of confusion, it is not surprising that efforts would be made to draw together, to organize, to give shape to the course offerings and the programs on individual campuses. I therefore included this question in my written survey: "Within the past ten years, have there been major changes in your program?" Of the 44 respondents 36 answered yes, 8 no. I interviewed 32 of the affirmative respondents, and each of them confirmed and explained the major changes that had been made. Of the respondents who reported no major changes in their programs, most said during interviews or in notes on the questionnaire that there had been relevant changes on campus or that important changes were then being planned. (Note: Throughout this report, as here, I indicate any qualifications of the survey responses.) One director explained that a complete restructuring of the graduate program affected the writing program: it changed the patterns of graduate students' teaching assignments, resulted in more composition and fewer literature classes, reduced class size to twelve, and led to changes in curricula. Another reported no changes in the freshman program but explained that a new cross-curricular writing program had been set up. During interviews 3 said that their English departments were hiring writing program directors to fill newly created or redesigned positions. Another 2 indicated that they had begun planning changes, 1 because "computers have arrived."

To see what generated the changes that have already been made, I asked survey respondents for the information reported in table 1. In the programs

Table 1
Any or all of the following forces could have provided impetus for the creation or redesign of your program. Please identify the three or four strongest forces for change on your campus.

Forces for change	Number of responses
Faculty decisions, interests, or opinions	32
Students' needs, interests, or opinions	31
Administrative decisions, interests, or opinions	27
Developments in composition, rhetoric, or related fields	25
The example of other writing programs	12
Commission reports	2
Media coverage of education	2
Public opinion	1
Governmental actions, mandates, or interests	0
Other	4

Note: 38 responses.

studied, the strongest forces for change were found in the faculty, students, and administration and in composition, rhetoric, and related fields. Next in order, though with only half the number of responses (12 compared with 25), was the example of other writing programs. Only 2 respondents mentioned commission reports, and only 2 noted media coverage of education. One cited public opinion, and none marked governmental actions, mandates, or interests. Other factors were "new leadership in the program," "a new faculty member hired to prepare graduate assistants," "the composition program's effort to separate from the English department," and "alumni interests."

Surprisingly few seemed to look beyond their own campuses for explanations, though in interviews it became clear that outside forces did affect decisions. The strongest forces, which I asked respondents to identify, are simply those closest at hand. It seems that commission reports do not inspire change—within a discipline, across campus, or beyond—until they are espoused or taken into account by faculties, administrators, and students on individual campuses. We might have expected the example of other writing programs to rank higher on the list of reported influences. A few comments during interviews indicated some impetus from other programs—"We knew about the Michigan model," for instance, or, "We adopted the plan for a mentor system that Ed Corbett had devised"—but again the forces closest to home seem to be the strongest. Note too that respondents added another category of influence: leadership, new or emergent ("a new faculty member hired to prepare graduate assistants").

The next question in my survey was, "When did these changes occur?" Several respondents replied, "At various times," or "Continually." Others said, "Since 1976," "Since 1978," or "1979-82." Looking for the point at

Table 2
Years When Changes Were Initiated

Year	Number of responses	Year	Number of responses
1974	2	1980	5
1975	0	1981	4
1976	2	1982	5
1977	3	1983	5
1978	7	1984	1
1979	7		

which change was initiated, I tabulated the responses by marking the first years named by the 41 respondents who gave dates. The results are shown in table 2. It seems that 1978 and 1979 were peak years and that, while changes initiated then have continued, the eighties have also seen changes introduced each year. (Because the survey was mailed in October 1984, this chart does not reflect all changes introduced during the 1984-85 academic year: there might well have been more responses for 1984 if the survey had been done later in the year.)

Studying this time of expansion and change, I asked those I interviewed to describe the changes on their campuses. A few said that change had been gradual, given increasing enrollments and new understandings of how to teach writing. At least 2 departments have introduced or strengthened technical- and business-writing programs and seen them expand dramatically. Upper-division courses and requirements have been added or modified. Most schools have begun emphasizing advanced courses, though 1 has moved from a vertical requirement (one-quarter courses required in the freshman, sophomore, and junior years) to a horizontal one (a three-quarter sequence in the freshman year). Many schools have initiated programs or courses for writing across the curriculum, some with outside funding.

In addition to altering undergraduate courses, often extensively, many programs have begun focusing on graduate instruction. They have created or modified their training programs for teaching assistants, and some have also created degree programs in writing or rhetoric. This recognition of writing as a field of study is sometimes reflected in faculty appointments and promotions.

Some of the most dramatic changes have accompanied the appointments of new directors or faculty members interested in writing. In the past ten years (primarily within the past five) a good number of the directors responding have accepted positions in the universities surveyed, as have other key faculty members in English and composition. Equally dramatic are the effects of creating new programs—such as those at Michigan; Minnesota, Minneapolis; and UCLA.

Narrowing the focus to the past five years, we can see in more detail the kinds of changes that have recently been made. I asked respondents to iden-

Table 3
Over the past five years, in which areas has your writing program changed?

	Number of Responses			
	Type		Number	
Area	New	Modified	Increased	Decreased
Courses, programs, or services				
Preparatory	0	12	12	2
Introductory	0	16	12	2
Intermediate	1	9	6	0
Advanced	1	19	19	0
Graduate	3	17	18	0
Faculty	1	5	6	0
Schools	1	2	3	0
Positions				
Administrative	1	14	9	1
Faculty	1	14	21	1
Clerical	1	10	11	2
Requirements				
Campuswide	1	14	14	0
Divisional	0	4	3	0
Departmental	0	5	5	0
Examinations	0	10	6	4
Instruction				
Courses	0	20	18	0
Seminars	0	10	9	0
Workshops	2	9	12	1
Tutorials	2	11	12	0
Students enrolled or participating				
For credit	0	15	24	1
For no credit	0	6	8	0
Support services	0	13	16	2
Additional resources				
Computer programs	4	13	17	0
Videotapes	1	2	5	0
Television programs	0	0	0	0
Audio programs	0	0	0	0
Other self-paced learning materials	0	3	2	0

Note: 40 responses.

tify areas in their programs that have altered during that time. As table 3 shows, the respondents indicated changes in both number and type. Most respondents reported that the elements of programs have changed in type and increased in size. More courses, workshops, and tutorials, as well as seminars, are now given. The greatest expansion has been in advanced and graduate courses: writing programs are spreading across campus, and the

Table 4
Within the past five years, how has your budget changed?

Type of change	Number of responses
Marked increase	18
Slight increase	17
No change	3
Slight decrease	3
Marked decrease	0

Note: 41 responses.

training of TAs and writing specialists is gaining attention. There are more faculty positions and also more administrative and clerical positions. Obviously, computers are gaining a place in these programs.

These changes have been supported by increases in funding, as table 4 indicates. Over the last five years, almost all programs surveyed have seen increases in their budgets, with a nearly equal balance between marked and slight increases. Most universities reporting marked increases have set up, or continued developing, ambitious programs, often hiring new faculty members, administrators, or office staff. Some have received grants or special increases in university funding; others indicated that their budgets have increased because of expanding enrollments or conversion to the semester system. Many reporting slight increases also have new or developing programs; some indicated that their budgets have increased because of inflation. Of those reporting no change, 1 had begun receiving generous funding earlier, 1 has a freshman program associated with a new cross-curricular program, and another has a new program. Of those reporting a slight decline, 1 had an established and well-funded program before this five-year period began, 1 noted a decline "in constant dollars," and 1 offered no additional comment.

These increases in funding, whether from internal or external sources, show how much attention writing has been given recently. They have supported the appointments and administrative changes I've begun to describe. Of course, funding alone doesn't explain transformations in writing programs: those transformations have depended on the people making them, the field of study developing to support them, and the universities endorsing them. As we have seen, the impetus for change has most often come from within the university, reflecting the interests and needs of students, faculty, and administration. Accordingly, a study of writing programs becomes a study of institutional change, a subject so complex that it can be treated in many ways. To approach the issue, let me outline what I've heard about the elements of change, then explain briefly how these elements seem to fit together.

Of the 44 programs in my survey, 36 have undergone major changes within the last ten years. Certainly, not all programs have changed equally or in the same ways, and not all innovations have succeeded. But writing programs have been and are being transformed, and the directors I interviewed spoke openly about the changes on their campuses. A mosaic of their comments will indicate some of the occasions for change they described. Because all changes—in structures, procedures, and staff—occur within particular university contexts, they depend on the support of faculty members and administrators and reflect the traditions, conventions, and resources of their universities.

During interviews, the directors described various circumstances and opportunities that have been associated with the changes in their programs:

Educational reform.   At North Carolina, Chapel Hill, a review of the entire undergraduate curriculum led to a reaffirmation of the composition requirement. The writing requirement at Minnesota, Minneapolis, was modified to include upper-division work at a time when the College of Liberal Arts was introducing changes in its curriculum. Clark initiated writing across the curriculum during a reorganization of the full introductory program for freshmen. The cross-curricular program at Penn receives strong administrative support because it fits clearly within the university's goals for the eighties. At Chicago, a report urging that graduate students be prepared as both scholars and teachers helped pave the way for graduate students who had been teaching in the Advanced Professional Writing program (the "Little Red Schoolhouse") to become writing assistants to regular faculty members teaching in the freshman Common Core Humanities program.

A tradition of liberal education.   At Chicago, a particular commitment to liberal education and undergraduate research has characterized the university since the Hutchins era. At Brown, the practice of treating writing courses as electives "fits the philosophy [and] tradition of this university," known for its open education. At Washington University as well, students' freedom to enroll in courses they choose is part of "the general freshman environment." Catholic University, which hired Jean Moss as director of rhetoric and composition, takes "a classical view of liberal education."

The character of the university.   Many directors explained that their programs are appropriate for their own institutions. They described their universities variously as "committed to a humanistic education," "small and institutionally conservative," "the most decentralized of [a state university's] campuses," or "ruthlessly democratic."

Association with a successful program.   The sophistication and success of the junior writing program at Maryland, College Park, influenced the English department's decision to regard composition as a field equal to others in decisions on promotion and tenure. At Washington University, writing courses have successfully been attached to intensive yearlong seminars available through FOCUS, an optional program for freshmen. As a result, the structure and content of writing courses outside that program have now been modified. The strength of Chicago's Little Red Schoolhouse helped prepare the way for other writing programs by training graduate students from a variety of academic fields, making the program seem an all-university project rather than one based entirely in the English department.

Support of the administration. From the beginning Michigan's dean and academic vice-president have lent their support to the university's English Composition Board (ECB). Jay Robinson, chair of the ECB, considers the crucial questions to be "those of institutional support." When William Schaefer left his position as executive director of the Modern Language Association to become UCLA's executive vice-chancellor, he had the intention of giving UCLA prominence in writing. At the same time, Richard Lanham was prepared to move from UCLA's English department into a writing program that he would help design. Tulane's new field of study— language, rhetoric, and writing—was established with the support of two deans and of the faculty, who recognized changes in the profession.

Support of the English department chair. At North Carolina, Chapel Hill, Erika Lindemann relies on strong endorsement from the chair of the English department. Peshe Kuriloff at Penn describes the support of the chair as essential. Another director explains that during his first two years in the program he depended on a "benevolent conspiracy" with the chair of the department and the director of graduate study.

Support of faculty members in English. The interdisciplinary writing program at Yale resulted from the efforts of key faculty members in English, supported by key administrators. When I interviewed directors from Iowa; Maryland, College Park; Minnesota, Minneapolis; and Pittsburgh, each of them named individual faculty members whose commitment to teaching and publishing in the field has greatly strengthened the program. One mentioned that the "history and seniority" of those working in composition have been important in helping to earn the program a strong reputation on campus.

Theory and research. The Program in Composition and Communication at Minnesota, Minneapolis, is accepted on campus as a solid program, "grounded in research." At Chicago, the advanced writing course is a "substantial theoretical course," and its structure "directly derives" from programs developed for professional organizations. Recent changes in Oregon's program have been philosophical, rather than structural, the curriculum having been redesigned within existing structures. In commenting on writing programs he respects, John Gage said he looks for programs that are "philosophically consistent."

Support of other departments. The College of Arts and Sciences at Indiana, Bloomington, resolved four years ago that an upper-level writing course should be required. The junior program at Maryland, College Park, was initially funded by departments outside English. Before a cross-curricular program was established at Clark, the faculty had voted that English should not hold full responsibility for writing. At USC, graduate students from many disciplines teach freshman composition, and departments view the Freshman Writing Program as a means of supporting their graduate students. This assistance has positively influenced the number and quality of students in some programs.

General goodwill. At Yale, the interdisciplinary writing program works effectively, its relationship with faculty members in the English department being one of "general goodwill." The programs on the Minneapolis and St. Paul campuses of the University of Minnesota have an informal and cooperative relationship. On another campus, the freshman program is well respected by the department: "I've worked hard on the politics of that." The director at another state university explains, "I have the power of gentle persuasion only."

Timing and circumstance. At Iowa, though the School of Journalism offers courses of its own, the English department created a course in extended prose (that is, the prose of free-lance journalism) through "local accident." On another campus, the freshman rhetoric program is related to the division for business and technical writing by "logistic necessity"; graduate students often teach business and technical writing, as well as freshman rhetoric, and these divisions are housed in the same building. At a private university, important funding resulted from "a chance remark to the president." A new program at one university had this beginning: "three of us were playing pool one night. . . ."

Leadership. One category remains, one that was not so much reported as demonstrated during interviews and campus visits: the impressive leadership given the writing programs. Some directors, as I've said, were hired specifically for this work; others moved into their administrative positions from faculty appointments they continue to hold. What's striking is not just their record of accomplishment but also the combination of patience and imagination behind it. The directors I interviewed displayed the critical intelligence needed in teaching writing together with the presence and understanding their administrative jobs demand. This entire report should be taken as a testimony to their achievement.

Having repeated and categorized what the directors have told me about the elements of change in their programs, I should attempt to draw these factors into some order. It's tempting, of course, simply to reorganize the list and say, "This is what it takes to create a sound writing program and secure its place in the university: a tradition of liberal education; a spirit of educational reform; the support of the administration, the department chair, and faculty members in English, as well as in other departments; grounding in theory and research; association with a successful program; general goodwill; fortunate timing and circumstance; and energetic, creative, solid leadership. Nothing easier. Except in real life. In real life, writing programs—and all other academic programs—depend on half, rather than full, measures of support. You might even say that any program with strength in each of the areas identified above could finally be expected to suffer, perhaps from some dulling entropy or at least from its uniqueness in the academic world.

In fact, programs succeed because they have some of the characteristics cited, not all of them. (One director remarked, "So much depends on having the right chair and the right dean at the right time.") What matters is the combination, the balance, the relative strength of these means of support. If every one of them existed in equal measure, we would need only builder's plans: assuming that quality materials would be at hand for talented artisans and skilled artists to use, there would be, enticingly, an inevitability to this work. As it is, we find odd combinations that work and chance associations that bring the right people together to talk about the right issues at the right time. Sometimes, of course, we find grand schemes and daring leaders who serve their departments and their universities well, all things seeming to conspire together for their success. But, as I argue at every point, no single model, no single prescription will work in all cases. Most important is the suitability of any single plan, the fit between any program and its university.

Having argued for diversity, I need now to explain why in the remainder of part 1 I present a composite of the programs I have studied. There are several reasons. First of all, even if a program is crafted for, or derived from, its particular circumstances, the decisions made about its design have implications for those designing other programs. Because composition as a field of study and instruction is changing and because the relation between composition and English studies (as well as that between writing programs and English departments) is uneasy, individual decisions occur within a national context and have the potential for influencing contemporary debates. Second, there are patterns to the changes that are now occurring within individual writing programs. While this point is closely related to the first, it differs from it in this way: while patterns may result from or effect intellectual or administrative changes in the endeavor, these patterns are also interesting in and of themselves, as an indication of how writing programs are—or were in one academic year—being administered across the country.

While viewing all programs together blurs their particularity, seeing each one alone can limit our understanding of it. Consequently, and third, all of part 1 serves as preparation for three case studies: the lines and the tones of the programs at North Carolina, Chapel Hill, at Penn, and at Harvard will emerge more clearly against the background of programs at various schools. Reciprocally, however, close study of these three programs will extend our appreciation of all those represented here.

CHAPTER 2

Administrative Structures

WRITING PROGRAMS RESIST being pressed into categories, each one being tailored to or resulting from its particular circumstances. To make a simple classification, I asked in my survey, "Does one academic unit offer or coordinate all instruction in English composition on your campus?" In response, 29 said yes, 12 no. Of those replying positively, 20 (about two-thirds) named the English department or a writing program within it as the unit responsible for writing instruction. This group includes the following campuses:

Brown	Maryland, College Park
Carnegie-Mellon	Missouri, Columbia
Case Western Reserve	North Carolina, Chapel Hill
Catholic	Oregon
Chicago	Penn
Duke	Pittsburgh
Illinois, Urbana	Purdue
Indiana, Bloomington	Stanford
Iowa State	Tulane
Kansas	Virginia

Others answering yes cited various administrative structures, some created specifically for their programs. At UCLA, the writing program combines a subdepartment of English and an independent office under the name UCLA Writing Programs. The following campuses have independent writing programs:

Harvard: Program in Expository Writing
Minnesota, Minneapolis: Program in Composition and Communication; St. Paul: Department of Rhetoric
MIT: MIT Writing Program
USC: Freshman Writing Program

At California, San Diego, each of the four residential colleges has an independent writing program, and the program directors meet in committee.

At Yale, the writing program is advised by an interdisciplinary faculty committee reporting to the dean of Yale College. At Clark and at Vanderbilt, writing-across-the-curriculum programs are administered through deans' offices. The program at Clark, for example, has from its start been supervised by the dean and assistant dean of the college, in conjunction with a faculty committee (Leone C. Scanlon, letter to the author, 4 Nov. 1985).

By contrast, no single unit holds full responsibility for writing instruction at 12 other schools:

California, Berkeley	Michigan State
Caltech	Nebraska, Lincoln
Colorado, Boulder	Princeton
Iowa	Rochester
McGill	Washington University
Michigan	Wisconsin, Madison

Various programs and departments, then, offer writing instruction on these campuses. At Michigan, the English department's Program in Composition offers freshman as well as advanced writing courses, and the English Composition Board coordinates the ambitious writing-across-the-curriculum program at the upper-division level. At Iowa, freshman writing is taught in the Rhetoric Program, and advanced and graduate courses are taught in the English department, with still other courses being offered by journalism, communication studies, the Writer's Workshop, business, and law. California Institute of Technology offers writing as a separate subject only in the remedial writing program, though nearly all humanities courses emphasize writing. McGill is exceptional in offering no writing classes. Robert Lecker, the associate chair of English, explained to me that students enter McGill unusually well prepared.

Line of Reporting

Typically, program directors report to chairs or heads of departments— English departments in nearly all cases. In a small department, the director may not have an advisory committee. When Jean Moss came to Catholic University, the English department had a faculty of eight; it now has thirteen full-time faculty members, in addition to lecturers and TAs. Moss, then, does not need a committee. Similarly, at Brown, which has a relatively small faculty of thirty-five or so, DeWitt Allen reports to the chair and is responsible to the English Faculty Senate, "as any other faculty member would be." In some departments, informal or ad hoc committees offer support: at Nebraska, Lincoln, those teaching graduate courses in composition theory informally advise the director, and on a number of campuses ad hoc committees select texts or handle other specific assignments. If an advisory committee exists, the number of meetings varies with the needs of each term or year. Alternatively, an existing committee within the department may deal with matters related to composition. This may be an undergraduate or curriculum committee or a committee of administrators within the composition program. At Pittsburgh, for example, the committee consists of the director of composition and three associate directors. There the English department's entire curriculum, graduate and undergraduate, is overseen by the chair and a committee of program directors (composition, literature, creative writing, graduate).

In many departments, however, the program director is regularly advised by a standing departmental composition committee. At Tulane, for example, Les Perelman now chairs the Freshman English Committee, made up of the three language, writing, and rhetoric faculty members (including Perelman); the department chair; one English faculty member appointed by the chair; and a graduate student representative. Perelman brings administrative questions to the chair and takes up policy with this committee. When necessary, he advances the committee's decisions to the department's executive committee and on to the department. A recommendation to institute teaching evaluations for graduate students, for example, recently went to the department for approval.

Some composition committees actively influence the affairs of large writing programs. At Indiana, Bloomington, the committee includes the coordinators of basic skills, the literature and composition program, and the business- and professional-writing course; the coordinator of new TAs; the head of a special summer program; interested English faculty members (for example, the teacher of legal writing); graduate students serving as assistants to the director and to the coordinator of new TAs; and five other graduate students elected by their peers. Marilyn Sternglass consults the chair about budgetary questions (such as the number of sections of business and technical writing to be scheduled) and takes conceptual questions (about course format, for example) to the committee, which makes recommendations to the chair or to the department as a whole. If, as expected, the subcommittee on the literature and composition program wants to generate substantial changes, it must present its recommendations to the department.

A similar committee holds broad responsibility at Purdue. Its members include the directors of all writing programs (writing lab, developmental writing, business writing, technical writing, freshman composition), the director of English as a second language, the director of the Office of Writing Review (an office responsible for certain screening procedures), and two graduate students. This composition committee has a wide spectrum of responsibilities, ranging from evaluating TAs to numbering courses to conducting a special project to learn what writing assignments are made in other departments.

Because business extends beyond the department, some writing program directors stress that they work not only with the chair and certain departmental committees but also with other university administrators. Betty Bamberg, director of USC's Freshman Writing Program, reports to the dean of humanities through the chair of the Freshman Writing Program Policy Committee. John Gage, the director of composition at Oregon, reports to the department head but also deals directly with the dean of the College of Arts and Sciences at times. Though there are "some ambiguities," this arrangement works very well.

Directors report directly to deans in three types of situations: (1) *In programs directed by department heads.* Henry Silverman, chair of Michigan State's Department of American Thought and Language, reports to the dean, "like any other chair." (2) *In independent programs.* Kim Davis, who directs Berkeley's Subject A program, reports to the dean of humanities in the College of Letters and Science and to the financial dean. The line of reporting above them extends to the provost and dean of the college. Thomas Lyons, directing the College Expository Writing Program at Colorado, Boulder, reports to the dean of the College of Arts and Sciences. And Donald Ross, director of the Program in Composition and Communication at Minnesota, Minneapolis, reports to the dean of the College of Liberal Arts. (3) *In special circumstances.* As the new director of Princeton's basic expository writing course, Michael Robertson reports to the assistant dean of the college.

Two of the interdisciplinary programs studied are directed by deans. Leone Scanlon, director of the Writing Center at Clark, reports to the assistant dean of the college, who is the chief administrator of the writing-across-the-curriculum program. And Scott Colley, associate dean of Vanderbilt's College of Arts and Science, coordinates the cross-curricular program on that campus.

On campuses with two programs, separate lines of reporting exist, with various links possible between the two. In the English Composition Board at Michigan, Jay Robinson reports to the dean of literature, science, and the arts. The chair of the ECB is not necessarily from English: in fact, the board members would support appointing a chair from outside the department, given their interest in presenting the board as a college community. English faculty members cannot constitute the majority of the committee, though the chair of English is an ex officio member. The director of the English department's Program in Composition, William Ingram, reports to the chair of English and confers with the Introductory Composition Committee. On that committee are four or five faculty members appointed by the chair, five TAs elected by their peers, and a liaison member or two from the ECB.

One director described the relationship between the two writing programs on his campus as "clear and straightforward—when no one mucks it up with politics." The role of politics and circumstance in all these arrangements cannot be underestimated. Sometimes "the line of reporting is less important than who you're sitting next to in committee meetings." Because so much depends on relationships and shared histories, another director observed, it would be very difficult for anyone from outside the program to come in as director. Clearly, in every situation, a program needs not only an appropriate structure and appropriate practices but also open and well-used channels of communication.

Reviews

Reviews are one means of testing a program and adjusting its fit within the university. As difficult as it is to measure the results of writing instruction or to estimate a program's overall effectiveness, reviews are clearly necessary. They allow the program's faculty and administrators to examine the substance and structure of their program so that they can, with a broad view of their methods and purposes, initiate changes or reinforce current procedures. Further, should the university's administrators or faculty senate question the effectiveness or importance of a writing program, a review with acceptable results will show a program to be responsible and will allow it to continue with its work. The vexed issues of evaluation are being addressed by our professional organizations, by experts in the field, and by directors and faculty members on individual campuses.

On the campuses included in the survey, by far the largest number of reviews have been initiated within the writing programs themselves (see table 5). Academic reviews by faculty committees have been divided quite evenly between voluntary and mandatory assessments of the program, though those by outside reviewers have nearly all been mandatory. All but one of the administrative reviews by department chairs have been voluntary. Of the few reviews by executive officers half have been voluntary and half

Table 5
Over the past five years, which of the following program reviews have been conducted?

Type of review	Voluntary	Mandatory
Self-review	29	6
Academic		
By faculty committees	11	12
By outside reviewers	2	8
Administrative		
By a department chair	9	1
By an executive officer	4	4
Other (by funding agency)	0	1

Note: 39 responses.

mandatory. Most evaluations, then, have been requested, accepted voluntarily, or designed by those working in the program.

Funding

When asked to indicate the total amount of their writing programs' funding for 1984-85, 24 respondents cited specific figures, ranging from $45,000 to $2 million, but 14 others said that their programs had no separate budgets or that the costs could not be easily estimated. One person said that the amount of funding was confidential, and 5 did not respond to the question. (See table 6.)

Program directors report a wide range in the amount of responsibility they hold for their programs' budgets. Some have little or no control, while others have substantial control over finances. Respondents who do not handle their programs' finances offered these comments: "I'm not responsible day-to-day for the budget. I review the TAs, hiring and firing them and the few adjuncts we have." "As in most places, funding here is allocated by the vice chancellor to the college to the school to the department. I enter special pleas based on enrollments, term by term." One director observed that his program receives funding as needed: it has gradually expanded as enrollments have increased, but with no advance planning or notice, decisions being made at the time of registration. A director who schedules three hundred sections of freshman classes during the year remarked that he handles only $100, the budget for photocopying. And another, who does not see the budget, finds the lack of information and control to be "a major problem." Needing a computer for the writing workshop, he doesn't have the authority to order one.

Even within programs that are budgeted separately, directors have varying degrees of discretion in making financial commitments. And the programs themselves vary tremendously in size, scope, and extent of financial

Table 6
What are the sources of your program's funding?

Source of funding	Number of responses
University	36
State (public institution)	14
Federal contracts and grants	2
State contracts and grants	1
Private contracts and grants	
Corporate	2
Foundation	4
Individual	3

Note: 41 responses.

support. The director of one comprehensive program at a large state university observed that she considers responsibility for the program's budget essential, both for understanding and controlling the program and for maintaining her status in it.

Table 6 indicates the sources of funding reported by the survey respondents. While funding usually comes from the university or the state, grants have helped to support the work of several programs. Carnegie-Mellon; Minnesota, Minneapolis; and Pittsburgh have received funding for computer projects: Carnegie-Mellon from Buell, the Fund for the Improvement of Postsecondary Education (FIPSE), and the Pew Memorial Trust; Minnesota, Minneapolis, from FIPSE; and Pittsburgh from the Ford Foundation. Pittsburgh has also received local funding for work in the National Writing Project and other programs. Yale reports substantial external funding: the Expository Writing Program was established with funds from the Pew Memorial Trust, and the Bass family has now assumed support for the program, with supplementary funding coming from other alumni gifts and from temporary grants made by the Newhouse and Surdna foundations. Clark University, after holding a grant from the National Endowment for the Humanities, has assumed the costs of its cross-curricular writing program. (Funding for the Writing across the University Program at Penn is described in the case study, chapter 9.)

CHAPTER 3

Program Directors

BECAUSE DIRECTORS PLAY key roles in defining and sustaining their programs, it is essential to understand the positions they hold. Further, because directors provided the information presented here, it is important to have a sense of the perspectives they bring to their work and to this discussion of program administration. To assess the directors' positions and roles in their programs, I included in the survey and interviews a series of questions about their administrative and academic appointments; the terms and conditions of those appointments, including evaluations and released time; and administrative support.

Table 7 shows the titles held by the program directors surveyed. As the list of respondents in the Preface shows, directors fall into three categories: (1) those in charge of independent programs (such as the Program in Composition and Communication at Minnesota, Minneapolis, or the Freshman Writing Program at USC), (2) those acting as directors of composition within English departments (at Brown, Case Western Reserve, Oregon, and Pittsburgh, for example), and (3) those directing freshman or other programs within English departments (usually freshman English, composition, or rhetoric, but also first-year studies or freshman-sophomore English).

Table 7
What is your administrative title?

Title	Number of responses
Director	30
Chair or head	8
Coordinator	4
Other	2

Most of those serving as chairs or heads manage English or other departments (including the Department of Rhetoric at Minnesota, St. Paul, and the Department of American Thought and Language at Michigan State). One directs an independent writing program (the MIT Writing Program), and one chairs an interdisciplinary writing board (the English Composition Board at Michigan).

Those holding the title of coordinator are responsible for a cross-disciplinary program (Writing across the University and the Writing Center at Penn); for campuswide programs as well as a program within one of the four residential colleges on campus (Campus Writing Programs and Third College Writing

Program at California, San Diego); for an entry-level writing program (Subject A at California, Berkeley); and for writing courses within an English department (composition courses at Nebraska, Lincoln). Other respondents include the chair of a writing committee (at Vanderbilt) and the supervisor of freshman instruction (at Duke, one of the universities hiring a director during 1984–85).

All but 2 of the 44 respondents hold academic appointments. The exceptions hold appointments as director of a writing center and as senior program officer. The 42 with academic titles hold appointments in the departments indicated in table 8 (the responses total 43 because one person holds an appointment in English and writing). As we would expect, most appointments are in English, with a few in literature, writing, or rhetoric. Respondents holding appointments in other departments or programs identified them as Subject A, Expository Writing, the MIT Writing Program, and the UCLA Writing Programs.

Table 8
In what department is your academic appointment?

Department	Number of responses
English	34
Literature	2
Writing or composition	2
Rhetoric	1
Other	4

Most, but not all, of the 44 respondents have earned their PhDs in English, as table 9 shows. One person has done postdoctoral work in education, and one holds a PhL, a licentiate in philosophy. Only one person has not earned a PhD. Some respondents have MAs in fields other than English, including education, history, psychology, and rhetoric; and some report BA or BS degrees in biology, education, philosophy, and journalism.

Table 9
Doctoral Fields of Respondents

Field	Number of responses
English	32
English education	4
English and linguistics	1
History	3
Rhetoric	1
Linguistics	1
American civilization	1

Table 10 shows the academic ranks survey respondents held during 1984–85, and table 11 shows the number and percentage of men and women in each rank. An unusually high percentage of program directors in this set of institutions are professors or associate professors. Though the number might seem inflated because some directors are chairs, these respondents head English departments responsible for writing or manage departments designated as writing or rhetoric departments. Writing programs, then, are predominantly in the hands of associate or full professors, most of whom are men; the percentage of women increases only as we move down the academic ranks. This pattern, of course, is not uncommon in English – or other – departments; it is a matter of professional concern.

Table 10
Academic Ranks of Respondents

Rank	Number of responses
Professor	14
Associate professor	17
Assistant professor	5
Lecturer or instructor	3
Other: senior lecturer, adjoint, academic administrator	3

To assess the status and prospects of those holding assistant professorships or other academic titles, as well as those without academic titles, we need to consider the issue of tenure. Table 12 shows the types of appointments the respondents hold in this respect. Those tenured are professors, associate professors, and a senior lecturer. (The senior lecturer explains that his appointment carries no time limitation.) Those on the tenure track are assistant professors and an associate professor who left a tenured position to accept this appointment, in which she expects to regain tenure. Those holding annual appointments are lecturers, an adjoint faculty member, an academic administrator, and a senior program officer (nonacademic). The three-year appointment (also nonacademic) is held by the director of a writing center. And the five-year appointment is held by a lecturer and academic coordinator now in his second term.

Table 11
Distribution of Academic Ranks

Rank	Men Number	Men Percent of rank	Women Number	Women Percent of rank	Total Number	Total Percent of sample
Professor	13	93	1	7	14	32
Associate professor	12	71	5	29	17	39
Assistant professor	3	60	2	40	5	11
Other or no academic rank	4	50	4	50	8	18
Total	32	63	12	27	44	100

The length of time directors and chairs have held these positions varies considerably, as table 13 shows. One response of "more than ten" refers to time on the faculty rather than to time in the position of director (since the program involved was set up only in 1981). While other responses may also refer to academic rather than administrative positions, most seem accurate, given the other information I have from the survey and from interviews. We have, then, a large number of directors and chairs in their first year, a fairly even distribution of those in the next seven categories, from one year to seven (except for a low point at four years), and a few with nine or more years in these positions.

With such a range of experience and such a variety of appointments (from full professor through senior program officer), the directors and chairs studied here represent an interesting cross section of leadership in writing programs. The statistics on their rank and tenure, even their location, have begun changing already, as some face review for tenure and promotion and some have accepted appointments at other universities. All information reported here, however, is based on the appointments described during the year of the study, 1984–85.

Table 12
What type of appointment do you hold?

Type of appointment	Number of responses
Tenured	31
Tenure-track	6
Term, renewable	
One-year	5
Three-year	1
Five-year	1

As we have seen, nearly all respondents hold academic appointments, and as a result they go through the normal academic reviews. To learn how their administrative work is evaluated, I asked an open-ended question: "How and how often is your administrative work reviewed?" Table 14 indicates the responses to the second part of this question. Those whose work is reviewed annually include department chairs, program directors

Table 13
How many full years have you held this position?

Number of years	Number of responses	Number of years	Number of responses
None	9	Six	6
One	6	Seven	4
Two	4	Eight	0
Three	5	Nine	2
Four	1	Ten	0
Five	5	More than ten	2

Table 14
Frequency of Administrative Review

Frequency of review	Number of responses
Annually	14
Every two years	2
Every three years	4
Every five years	3
Other	17

Note: 37 responses.

and coordinators, and a dean. Four of them added explanatory comments: "Departmental interim tenure review." "Annually by department chair through reports. Every five years through departmental review committee." "We submit annual reports to the dean. . . . My department also reviews my work at least every two years." "The chair and I annually review my work and the needs of the program, but I view it as a friendly and informal review. Formally, my work is reviewed by a faculty committee every 3-5 years in the context of rank and tenure reviews (just as all faculty work is reviewed)."

Of those offering other responses, 8 described their reviews as informal. Some of their comments: "Only informally, except through program review." "Informally, irregularly. In response to specific questions, procedures, problems. By [department] head, dean, provost." For 3 others there is no formal review procedure (for example, "No regular review established, apart from periodic reviews of the whole department by a campus committee"). Four said that their administrative work is not reviewed or is reviewed only in connection with tenure and promotion.

Because nearly all respondents hold academic appointments, formal reviews are often directly associated with, or perhaps subsumed by, academic reviews. The lack of formal review, however, does not mean that program administrators are not exposed to judgment. One person who said that he is not reviewed except "on broader performance as a scholar and classroom teacher" added that "of course, steps would be taken" if he did not handle his job well. Another, the last in this category, described his review as continual: "The dean periodically requires information about program work. Continual review is transacted by means of budget proposals, requests for permission to hire, budget reviews, promotion cases. Additional review is carried out during weekly School Council meetings. There are dozens of mechanisms for all this."

If we see complexity or ambiguity in review procedures, or some overlap between administrative and academic reviews, we can expect to find similar difficulties in the jobs themselves. Writing program administrators, whether department heads or course coordinators, must manage their programs while maintaining their professional lives. Balanced, these responsibilities can be seen as complementary: a teacher and scholar may understand what kind of program serves students well. On the other hand, an exhausted administrator may not have time for research. While the talents and interests needed for academic and administrative appointments are not the same, program directors do have commitments in both areas. To see how these administrative appointments are defined and supported, I included in the survey and interviews several questions about committee service, released time, and administrative support.

Committee Service

The extent of a program director's administrative responsibility depends on the size and nature of the program, and this entire report is a study of

Table 15
How many university committees do you now chair?

Number of committees chaired	Number of responses
None	24
One	14
Two	2
Three	2
Four	1

Note: 43 responses.

Table 16
On how many other university committees do you now serve?

Number of additional committees	Number of responses
None	5
One	9
Two	7
Three	9
Four	6
Five	1
More than five	4

Note: 41 responses.

such responsibility. Simply to add one bit of information, about committee service, I included the survey questions indicated in tables 15 and 16. Though very few respondents chair more than one committee, most do serve on other committees, the number ranging from one to more than five. In fact, there's fairly even distribution among the number of committees on which respondents serve, though only 1 person serves on five. Note that 4 directors serve on more than five committees. They also chair committees, 3 of them chairing one each and 1 of them chairing three.

Released Time

The issue of released time is complex because of the variations in normal work load from campus to campus and in the size of the programs involved. To show some patterns in the relation of teaching to administration, let me summarize the assignments of nine associate professors whom I interviewed.

At two universities on the quarter system, normal course loads are six and eight courses per year, the assignment of eight including summer teaching. At seven universities on the semester system, normal loads vary between three and six courses per year. The associate professors I spoke with said they are released from one to three courses per year, representing 25% to 60% of a normal load. Most report that they are given 50% released time. They teach, as a result, anywhere from one course to six each year. (Those on the quarter system teach three or six courses during the year. Those on the semester system teach one, two, or three a year.)

Given the size and complexity of their programs, do directors find this released time adequate for their administration? Some do and some do not. Consider, however, that the director teaching three courses on the quarter system finds he does not have time to write as he would like to, and that another director teaches six courses, also on the quarter system, with his teaching assignments spread over the summer as well as the academic year. He does direct a much smaller program. The question of adequacy of released time clearly has to do with normal course load, the size and scope of the program, expectations, demands, and research interests.

Since most respondents hold academic appointments, and since all are in research universities, they need time for research in their fields of interest. Teaching is also important because it provides connections with students, teaching assistants, other faculty members, and the profession. Directors must know their students and student populations, they need to train and direct their teaching assistants, they have to guide and maintain credibility with their faculty, and they want their programs, their classrooms, to be informed by sound understandings of writing and writing instruction. Because of their responsibilities for curriculum and administration, they need to be in the classroom. Yet their other administrative demands are consuming.

As I spoke with directors about their work, I found that many have no time for their own writing and research. If they are to maintain their professional vitality, and if their programs are to benefit from their special interests, they need leave or released time for their own work.

Many directors are teaching graduate seminars in rhetoric and composition, usually as part of the training required for teaching assistants. They find this work important. One assistant professor said that he normally teaches three courses: a graduate seminar, a freshman course, and one other course. This seems to him a good balance. Another said that he regularly teaches a large course in the English department and that this assignment is valuable to him, particularly because it provides good public relations for his program.

Some directors receive released time for their work with TAs. Erika Lindemann, for example, annually receives a two-course release for her administration and a one-course release for her work in TA training (in a program with 100 TAs, 25 or 30 new each year). Leonora Woodman reports this arrangement: with a normal course load of six courses per year on the semester system, she receives a two-course release for administration and a one-course release for work with the TA mentor program in the fall and a one-course release for each in the spring. She considers this distribution of her time appropriate.

Administrative Staff

Because of the variations in the size of the programs and in the amount of support and funding given them, the size of the administrative staff also varies greatly. On one campus, the director works with office help only. He has one colleague, a regular faculty member, who does much of the work but does not hold an administrative position. In Berkeley's Subject A program,

Table 17
In which of the following areas do you need more or better support?

Area	Number of responses
Funding	28
Faculty development	24
Computers	
Hardware	20
Software	16
Research	16
Clerical work	14
Support services	14
Administration	12
Program evaluation	12
Equipment and supplies	11
Hiring and promotion	10
Curriculum design	8
Student data	7
Class scheduling	4
Testing	4
Texts and course materials	2
Handling grievances and complaints	2
None	2

Note: 42 responses.

Table 18
Areas Most in Need of Administrative Support

Area	Number of responses
Faculty development	11
Funding	10
Program evaluation	7
Hiring and promotion	6
Clerical work	5
Curriculum design	5
Computers	
Hardware	4
Software	4
Research	4
Administration	3
Equipment and supplies	3
Student data	3
Support services	1
Class scheduling	1
Testing	1
Texts and course materials	1
Handling grievances and complaints	1

Kim Davis has three experienced lecturers who assist him in training and supervising graduate student instructors but who receive no additional com-
pensation, except occasionally for special projects. At Purdue, Leonora
Woodman has a TA as acting assistant and excellent secretarial help, and
the administrative assistant to the department head handles all scheduling.
At Minnesota, Minneapolis, Donald Ross currently has the financial support to hire TAs for the equivalent of eight sections a year: they take on such
administrative assignments as directing the writing lab. In addition, various
faculty members take responsibility for individual courses or help supervise
training. At USC, Betty Bamberg receives support for the academic program from four staff assistants: the director for international students, the
director for evaluation and testing, the Writing Center director, and the
director of interdisciplinary writing. Twelve experienced instructors each
receive a one-course release to assist in training new instructors and coordinating classroom instruction.

Administrative Support

The areas in which program directors say they need more or better support
are listed in table 17. Funding is the most common need in the programs
studied. Next comes faculty development, which may refer to development
programs for writing or English faculty members (regular or temporary, full-
or part-time) or for faculty members in other departments. Third we find
computers, with hardware being named somewhat more frequently than
software. Support is also needed for research, which may include research
being done by the director or by the program's faculty.

In the next six items, receiving 10 to 14 responses, practical matters (clerical work, equipment and supplies) show up with programmatic concerns
(support services and program evaluation), along with administration and
staffing (hiring and promotion). Then there are two that match curriculum
(curriculum design) with administration (student data). The remaining
areas were not often cited as needing more or better support.

I asked respondents, after answering this question, to underline the two or
three areas of need that now seem most important to their programs. Thirty
respondents underlined at least one item. Table 18 indicates the areas they
gave priority. In this tabulation faculty development and funding reverse
positions. Program evaluation, hiring and promotion, clerical work, and
curriculum design advance; computers take a lower position; and support
services drop near the bottom.

The question of support drew one unusual, but rhetorically effective,
reply. In what areas do you need more or better support? "None: I have more
support, ideas, possibilities, experience than I could possibly put to use."

CHAPTER 4

The Writing Programs

TO LEARN THE SIZE AND SCOPE of the writing programs studied, I asked directors and chairs during interviews to estimate the number of sections scheduled and the number of students enrolled each year. Their responses were sometimes complicated because of the variety of courses and special programs offered: freshman, advanced, and graduate writing courses, as well as writing-intensive courses or workshops handled by consultants from writing programs. Variety, including a wide range in size, clearly characterizes this set of writing programs.

Let's consider first the profiles of some of the smallest programs. At Clark writing-intensive courses are offered across campus. In addition, the English department offers a section or two of basic writing and five to sixteen sections of intermediate writing each semester. Both courses, for those placed in them, are prerequisites to the cross-curricular course, and together they serve 300 students each year. Clark has an entering freshman class of 550.

Freshman writing courses at Catholic University enroll 450 students in the fall and another 200 in the spring; six junior writing courses enroll another 100 students or so. The total number enrolled in writing classes, 750, slightly exceeds the number entering as freshmen, 700.

Of Princeton's 1,100 entering freshmen, some 800 enroll in any of eight designated courses, ranging in size from 40 to 400. The precepts (discussion sections) for these courses are limited to 14 students each. Another 250 students enroll in a class called The Craft of Writing, and at the time of the survey a few students were exempt from the writing requirement.

By contrast, consider the profile of the largest program included in this study. To allow Michigan State's 6,000 to 6,700 entering freshmen to satisfy a three-quarter (nine-credit) writing requirement, the Department of American Thought and Language (ATL) offers more than 200 sections of its writing courses each term. With the class size at 28, some 5,600 students enroll each term, totaling 16,800 enrollments during the year. The chair, Henry Silverman, estimates that this program serves 90% of the freshmen at Michigan State.

These figures are humbling when compared with the corresponding statistics for other campuses. Most programs, of course, fall between the two extremes represented by Michigan State on the one hand and Clark, Catholic, and Princeton on the other. Table 19 suggests the size of various programs by citing the estimated number of sections scheduled during the year. The number of students enrolling in these sections, of course, varies from campus to campus. The extremes in class size reported during interviews were 12 at Washington University ("My predecessor has the credit for that") and 28 at a large state university. Variations within a single program can be represented by those at Tulane and UCLA. While most freshman classes at Tulane enroll 23 students, the advanced freshman classes, for students receiving SAT verbal scores of 600 or better, are limited to 15. At UCLA, class size varies from 25 in the required freshman course to 20 in the preceding course and all advanced courses and to 14 in special preparatory courses. Thus in special circumstances (for added preparation or honors work) classes may be reduced to the size appropriate for seminars, and upper-division classes may be kept smaller than required freshman classes. The range of class sizes cited in interviews is suggested, in broadest outline, in table 20.

Table 19
Sections of Writing Courses Scheduled Annually

Campus	Number of sections	System: quarter or semester
Maryland, College Park	465	S
Iowa State	370	S
UCLA	365	Q
Nebraska, Lincoln	350	S
North Carolina, Chapel Hill	300	S
USC	300	S
Oregon	265	Q
Indiana, Bloomington	230	S
Virginia	187	S
Illinois, Urbana	145	S
Colorado, Boulder	110	S
Brown	93	S
Carnegie-Mellon	65	S

Courses, Programs, and Services

Because individual writing programs vary greatly in procedures and services, only a detailed study of each one could describe their complexities. Given my focus on administrative structures and processes, the questions I asked about the programs' offerings were more skeletal than substantive. Table 21 shows the responses to the first of these questions.

The courses and services of these programs are fairly broadly distributed among university students. Interviews suggested that by far the largest proportion of most programs is devoted to freshmen. (The person not responding to this question described a freshman program during an interview. Thus, all but one of the programs studied have courses or services for freshmen: at Iowa, the freshman courses are offered by the Rhetoric Program.) Yet, the programs studied do serve students at all levels, half of them offering courses, programs, and services for graduate students. Just under a fourth of the writing programs and departments represented here have programs for faculty members or for students or teachers in the local schools. During interviews, comments on schools programs showed a wide range: some directors mentioned strong programs associated with the National Writing Project; others said that they have been encouraged to work seriously with the schools but that, given the demands on their time and the pressures of earning tenure or promotion, they have not yet been able to do so.

Table 20
Average Class Size

Campus	Number of students
Colorado, Boulder	25
Oregon	23
Purdue	23
Illinois, Urbana	22
Michigan (Composition Program)	22
Nebraska, Lincoln	22
North Carolina, Chapel Hill	22
Maryland, College Park	20
Pittsburgh	20
Michigan (English Composition Board freshman tutorials)	16
Princeton	14

To serve the populations identified above, the programs studied teach writing through the various types of courses and offerings classified in table 22. In addition to courses, seminars, and workshops classified generically as teaching writing, 25 programs offer instruction in the teaching of writing and 19 in composition theory. In about half the programs, offerings include literature (22), rhetoric (20), and creative writing (20), followed by English as a second language (18). Next in order are business writing (17), technical writing (17), and then scientific writing (14). About one-fourth (11) of the programs now offer writing-enrichment or -intensive courses, made available in various departments. Slightly

Table 21
For whom are your courses, programs, and services designed?

Students	Number of responses
Freshmen	42
Sophomores	32
Juniors	32
Seniors	28
Graduate students	22
Faculty members	10
Students or teachers in local schools	9

Note: 43 responses.

fewer programs teach journalism (10), other professional writing (9), or linguistics (9). Only 6 teach legal writing and 2 communications.

Writing centers or laboratories are available on 28 campuses. (For excellent discussions of writing centers, see Olson.) Tutorials of several types are also available: drop-in (16), by appointment (16), and regularly scheduled (11), as well as full-term, either elective or required (4 each). Though tutorials may be offered through writing centers, some campuses have developed special tutorial programs, described in chapter 5. Among learning resources, computers rank clearly at the top of the list (15), with videotapes and audiocassette materials next in order (6 each).

Table 22
How is writing taught in your program?

Type of service	Number of responses
Courses, seminars, or workshops	
Writing	43
Writing-enrichment or -intensive	
(offered in various departments)	11
Business writing	17
Technical writing	17
Scientific writing	14
Legal writing	6
Journalism	10
Other professional writing	9
Teaching of writing	25
Composition theory	19
Rhetoric	20
Literature	22
Creative writing	20
Linguistics	9
Communications	2
English as a second language	18
Tutorials	
Full-term, required	4
Full-term, elective	4
Regularly scheduled	11
By appointment	16
Drop-in	16
Writing center or laboratory	28
Learning resources	
Computer programs	15
Videotapes	6
Television programs	2
Audiocassette materials	6
Other self-paced learning	
materials	3
Other: workshops, workbooks and	
instructors' materials, reading	
and library programs	3

Note: 43 responses.

Writing Requirements

Several universities report no writing requirement. "Open education is a selling point" at Brown, where writing courses are "very popular" and only a few students are held for remedial work in writing. Penn also has no writing requirement in the School of Arts and Sciences (see ch. 9). Catholic requires only students with SAT verbal scores below 550 to take a writing course. At Colorado, Boulder, writing courses are mandatory for students in some professional schools (business, environmental design, pharmacy), but for 12,000 out of 20,000 students, there is no requirement.

Most universities surveyed require at least one freshman writing course. Washington requires a semester; Tulane requires two. At Purdue, the requirement is two semesters for all but engineering students. Students who qualify for a course for those with superior writing skills can satisfy the requirement in one semester. At USC, the requirement is flexible, from none to three semesters: 90% of the students take two semesters.

Vanderbilt has an alternative type of writing requirement. At Vanderbilt, students must take two designated "W" (writing-intensive) courses within their first four semesters. Scott Colley explains that a "course carries a 'W' if the instructor (1) assigns 20–25 typescript pages; (2) requires at least five papers; (3) offers two obligatory tutorials with each student; (4) demands that several papers be recast and rewritten; and (5) devotes a certain amount of class time to a discussion of writing, rhetoric, logic, and other appropriate topics which concern students of writing" (letter to the author, 13 Dec. 1984). These courses satisfy the writing requirement for most Vanderbilt students: only those needing further help are held for English Composition in addition to the two required W courses.

Vanderbilt's writing-intensive courses are like those usually offered as upper-division writing requirements at other universities. Michigan's English Composition Board is well known for its pioneering efforts to integrate writing into existing junior and senior courses. Sometime during their last two years Michigan students must take one ECB-approved course emphasizing writing (see Morris for a description of this program). Indiana, Bloomington, also requires students to take an upper-level writing-intensive course offered in one of many departments. Alternatively, Maryland, College Park, requires students to take a self-standing advanced writing course (see Kinneavy and the discussion of writing across the curriculum, below).

Table 23
When were the statements of your program's principles and goals prepared?

When prepared[a]	Number of responses
This year	8
Last year	14
Two years ago	9
Three years ago	8
Four years ago	4
Five years ago	7
More than five years ago	8

[a]One respondent checked all categories and said that statements were updated annually.

Principles and Goals

To learn how program directors develop or maintain control over curricula and programs, I asked a series of questions about written materials: statements of principles and goals, syllabi, and texts. Again, the questions are not comprehensive. They simply reveal whether or not these particular means of control are commonly used. When asked whether their programs had written statements of principles and goals, 37 survey participants said yes, 5 said no, and 2 did not respond. Those who answered yes were asked when and by whom these written statements were prepared; tables 23 and 24 show the responses.

Most programs do have written statements of principles and goals, most often prepared by program administrators but also by faculty committees and faculty members. The largest number were prepared in the year before that of the survey, though the dates they were prepared range from the year being studied through more than 5 years earlier.

Table 24
Who prepared the statements of your program's principles and goals?

Preparers[a]	Number of responses
Program administrators	28
Faculty	
Committee(s)	15
Member(s)	10

[a]Some respondents said that administrators and faculty members prepared the statements together.

Syllabi

Like written statements of principles and goals, syllabi are a means of exerting control over the form, as well as the content, of courses. This effort at prediction and control can be exerted at two levels, that of the individual classroom and that of the program. Understanding that classes can—and frequently should—vary from plans announced at the beginning of any term and that syllabi can themselves be relatively open or relatively closed, I asked several questions about the development and use of syllabi in writing programs.

Responses to the first question, "Do you provide syllabi for some or all

Table 25
If you provide syllabi for some courses, how are they generally used?

	Number of responses	
Use	For some instructors	For all instructors
Sample	4	11
Recommended	5	6
Required	8	7

of your courses?" show that most, but not all, programs do provide syllabi for their courses: 34 survey participants said yes, 7 said no, and 3 did not reply. This question was followed by questions on the use and preparation of the syllabi, addressed separately to those who provide syllabi for only some courses (tables 25 and 26) and to those who provide them for all courses (tables 27 and 28).

Table 26
If you provide syllabi for some courses, who prepares them?

Preparers	Number of responses
Program administrators	18
Faculty committees	6
Individual instructors	23
Other: faculty and graduate-student subcommittees, graduate students for PhD requirement, program administrators with senior teaching assistants (graduate students)	3

Table 27
If you provide syllabi for all courses, how are they generally used?

	Number of responses	
Use	For some instructors	For all instructors
Sample	2	5
Recommended	0	4
Required	1	3

If we look back over the responses to questions about syllabi and those about statements of principles and goals, some patterns emerge. Very nearly the same number of respondents provide syllabi for some or all courses (34) as have written statements describing their programs' principles and goals (37). Further, the number of respondents saying that program administrators prepare the written statements (28) is nearly equaled by the combined total of those preparing syllabi for some or all courses (27). As we would expect, individual instructors more frequently prepare the syllabi (a combined total of 29) than prepare the program's statements (10), and more faculty committees prepare statements (15) than prepare syllabi for instructors (a combined total of 7).

Table 28
If you provide syllabi for all courses, who prepares them?

Preparers	Number of responses
Program administrators	9
Faculty committees	1
Individual instructors	6

Texts

Following the questions about syllabi, I asked a question about text selection. Table 29 shows the pattern of response. Nearly as many individual instructors select texts as prepare syllabi, and faculty committees are somewhat more commonly involved in choosing texts than in preparing statements of principles and goals. But far fewer program administrators handle text selection than prepare either syllabi or statements on the program.

Table 29
Who selects the texts for your courses?

Selectors	Number of responses
Program administrators	12
Faculty committees	18
Individual instructors	27
Other	2

Note: 42 responses.

Though administrators do not often choose texts, some have written texts that influence the courses taught. As table 30 shows, texts written by members of the faculty or administrative staff are used in 23 of the programs studied. In the remaining programs, it may be that such texts are not adopted or, very simply, that none are available. The use of texts written within the program shows that the program's director or teachers are involved in this professional field and that their research and writing are helping to shape the program conceptually and pedagogically. The question of what freedom instructors have in selecting or using these texts is related to that of how syllabi and statements of principles and goals are developed and used. These questions, of course, escape a written survey.

Table 30
Are texts written by members of your faculty or administration used in the program?

Response	Number of responses
No	20
Occasionally	14
Often	2
Every term	7

Note: 43 responses.

Writing across the Curriculum

In response to the question "Is your program responsible for writing across the curriculum?" 18 survey participants said yes, 25 said no, and 1 did not reply. One director asked, "Does this [question] mean only one thing?" Certainly, neither "writing across the curriculum" nor "responsibility for it" means only one thing. Yet, remarkably, writing across the curriculum has very quickly become identifiable as a concept and, often, as a program. James L. Kinneavy comments, "In a short time (much less than it took Piaget, for instance), writing across the curriculum has been entered in the list of descriptors for bibliographic searches for the ERIC system [Educational Resources Information Center]" (13). Nearly 41% of the respondents describe their programs as responsible for writing across the curriculum.

"Writing across the curriculum" may be a general notion that writing should be stressed in many disciplines or an informed conviction that writing cannot be separated from knowing and that the study and practice of writing will contribute to learning in all disciplines. Similarly, the use of writing throughout the university curriculum can be encouraged informally or instituted more dramatically through workshops, courses, and special programs. (See Kinneavy's and Cullen's articles for descriptions of several types of programs.) Because any effort to emphasize writing will be grounded in the politics and allegiances of faculty members, departments, and campuses, there is no simple correlation between the complexity of the idea and the sophistication of the practice. A leader in the field of composition, someone committed to the principles of writing across the curriculum, may not find an ambitious program right for a particular campus. Further, no single model can be developed to serve all campuses. Reports from individual programs, then, suggest both how writing across the curriculum is developing as an idea, or a set of ideas, and how it is taking shape on various campuses.

On some campuses, program directors do not feel the need, or have not found the means, for cross-curricular efforts. At Tulane, a small university, Les Perelman recently found through a faculty survey that no special program is needed: students are now writing in classes across campus. At Iowa, Richard Lloyd-Jones would like funding for a new effort, but he doesn't expect this state university's finances to improve. He says that when the Liberal Arts College considers writing across the curriculum, the possible cost seems forbidding. On the other hand, the English department's writing courses, always filled by the midpoint of registration, enroll large numbers of prelaw and premed students. The department does offer courses in business and science writing, and various other writing programs have been set up independently. Similarly, Purdue, with nine different schools on campus, has not yet worked with writing across the curriculum, Leonora Woodman says.

But the writing program offers an unusually wide range of courses, including special sections of its advanced course that focus on scientific and, beginning in 1985-86, legal writing.

In the middle range, other schools are just now setting up programs or hope to do so. At Minnesota, St. Paul, interested faculty members who meet over lunch each month have begun emphasizing writing in their classes, and the rhetoric department is experimentally combining its advanced writing course with senior seminars in the College of Forestry and the Department of Agronomy. At Catholic University, faculty members seem to have a renewed interest in writing across the curriculum, and a model was being planned within the honors program during the spring of 1985. And at USC, writing across the curriculum is "just developing," with adjunct courses being designed at advanced levels. This effort follows the revival of an earlier interdisciplinary freshman program: there students can register for a general-education lecture course and coregister for a composition course taught by an instructor with expertise in the discipline of the content course. Reading and writing assignments in the coregistered composition course are related to topics and assignments in the general-education course.

Clearly, elements of what might be considered writing-across-the-curriculum programs inhere in many writing programs and on many campuses. Though the various courses and programs at Iowa may not have been shaped into a single program, and though the interdisciplinary features of the freshman program at USC haven't yet been extended through the upper division, writing escapes departmental confinement on both these campuses. Similarly, though Marilyn Sternglass reports that Indiana, Bloomington, has "no writing-across-the-curriculum program," every student in the College of Arts and Sciences must take an upper-level course that has a substantial writing component and that is taught by a faculty member in the subject area. This junior-level requirement is often considered fundamental to a writing-across-the-curriculum program. Here again we see the problem—or the challenge—of definition: both the meaning and the implications of "writing across the curriculum" are still being explored.

Before we turn to some of the programs that identify themselves as responsible for writing across the curriculum and that seem to have developed the structure and the philosophy to support their efforts, let me place these positive examples in perspective by offering a contrasting study. One director reported that a cross-curricular program at a public university has failed. In the early seventies, given a new demand for writing courses, members of the English department appealed to the dean: the department would do its share if other departments would help staff the writing courses. A program was set up in 1976, based on the assumption that faculty members from other departments who wrote well themselves could teach others to write. But the program did not draw enthusiastic faculty participation, and it was hurt by staff cuts within the university. It was discontinued in 1982. According to the current director, the problems were that the basic assumption was faulty and that a number of teachers in the program were there by assignment rather than by choice.

Taking this program's failure as a caution, let me outline several varieties of writing-across-the-curriculum programs. In the context of this study, they might best be traced along a spectrum based on the levels at which they are offered and the ranks of their teachers or tutors.

At Clark, writing across the curriculum is part of an introductory program legislated by the faculty. Basic and intermediate writing courses are taught in the English department, and other courses emphasizing writing are taught in many departments. Undergraduates work as teaching assistants for groups of their peers enrolled in these courses, and the faculty members teaching these courses meet monthly "to educate [them]selves and advise the Dean." A writing center, funded and staffed by the undergraduate college, offers noncredit workshops and tutoring.

Vanderbilt's freshman program in English is supplemented by W (writing-intensive) courses offered in English and other departments. Students must take two W courses during their first four semesters. Faculty members teaching these courses—and teaching assistants—are invited to workshops taught by the associate dean of the College of Letters and Science, who chairs the Writing Committee. At the time of the survey, he was also preparing a handbook for these faculty members.

The graduate students who teach in Chicago's University Writing Programs are selected from the entire university, representing fields ranging from biological sciences to political science to theology. They start as lectors in Advanced Professional Writing (the Little Red Schoolhouse), leading small seminars composed of juniors and seniors from all concentration programs in the college. The next year these lectors become writing assistant interns in the freshman Common Core Humanities program or dormitory tutors for students in the Common Core Social Sciences program. After that training, they may become senior lectors in the Advanced Professional Writing program, working with graduate students from the School of Business or the School of Social Service Administration, or in adult professional programs offered by the Office of Continuing Education in the evenings or on weekends.

Michigan's English Composition Board screens all entering students and offers tutorials for those needing preparation for the introductory class offered by the English department. In addition, the board certifies and supports junior-senior writing courses in a variety of disciplines. All students must take one such course before graduation. The board offers seminars for those teaching the courses.

At Yale, graduate students from various disciplines teach writing-intensive sections of courses offered across campus at all levels. In addition, professional tutors work in the residences. Members of the English faculty continue to teach the writing courses offered in their department (Daily Themes, for example).

At UCLA, freshman writing courses introducing students to the varieties of academic discourse are taught by lecturers and TAs. Elective writing courses—intermediate, advanced, and graduate—are also taught by lecturers. These elective courses include special and adjunct sections for students enrolled in particular courses or majoring in certain fields.

The English department at Maryland, College Park, requires freshman writing courses, taught by graduate students, and junior writing courses, taught by part-time and regular faculty members. The junior courses are taught in four areas: humanities, natural science and technology, social science, and business. (The department also offers an MA in rhetoric, linguistics, and pedagogy and PhD areas in rhetoric and linguistics.)

Carnegie-Mellon offers, in addition to undergraduate writing courses and majors, graduate degrees in professional writing and rhetoric. The MA in professional writing includes the study of graphic design and computer studies, as well as rhetoric, linguistics, and technical writing. Courses are taught by faculty members and graduate students in English, as well as in psychology, computer science, and philosophy.

Degrees

Responses to the survey show that half the programs studied offer writing as a major field, minor field, or area of concentration at several degree levels, as shown in table 31. In interviews some directors offered explanations and comments on the degrees and concentrations available in various programs.

Since 1981, Purdue has accepted rhetoric and composition as a field for the PhD. Of the 38 MA and PhD students working in this graduate program in 1984–85, most were PhD candidates.

Table 31
For what degrees is writing offered as a major field, minor field, or area of concentration?

Degree	Number of responses
BA	14
BS	4
MA	11
PhD	14
None	16

Note: 38 responses.

Pittsburgh accepts composition as an area of concentration for the PhD in English, allowing students to write one of four exams in this area. In 1984–85, of 65 graduate students, 30 were MFA students; 20 of the remaining 35 were working in composition. To that date, 4 people had completed dissertations in composition and rhetorical theory, and 1 had a dissertation in progress. (Update in late 1985: the four-part area exams have been discontinued. "Students now, with the assistance of three faculty members, define a project leading to a paper and a written and oral exam. The goal is to eliminate what seemed to be divisions in English Studies [the 19th century, the romantics, composition]" [David Bartholomae, letter to the author, 6 Nov. 1985].)

At Indiana, Bloomington, a student may earn the PhD in English literature with a composition minor. This is a two-tiered program, with comprehensive written exams in one area and an oral as preparation for the dissertation. Students may write on composition theory. In addition, at the time of the survey, the university was considering (and has since begun) a PhD program in language, literature, and literacy. This program replaces the PhD in English language, a program that allowed students to take one area exam and the oral in composition and to write a dissertation on language.

Carnegie-Mellon has a PhD in rhetoric, an MA in professional writing, and an MA in literary theory, rhetorical theory, and creative writing. (In 1984, one student had already received the PhD in rhetoric; a second was scheduled to receive it at the end of 1985–86.) Carnegie-Mellon also offers three undergraduate majors in writing: creative, technical, and professional. All majors take a core of literary-cultural courses, then work in their selected areas.

Oregon includes rhetoric and composition as one of five areas for the PhD in English. Students may specialize in that field. At the time of the study, seven students were preparing dissertations on rhetoric and composition or on rhetorical criticism. Five had recently completed dissertations in these areas.

Virginia offers a PhD in language, literature, and pedagogy. This program is designed "to be broader than that for the research doctorate and to fit the needs of school and college English teachers" (program description).

Tulane accepts language, writing, and rhetoric as a minor field for the PhD and as a major field for the BA. Undergraduates take advanced writing courses and courses in the history of contemporary theories of rhetoric, linguistics, or the language, as well as courses in literature.

Iowa gives an MA in English with emphasis on expository writing. Students may use this work as the foundation for a doctoral program: composition can become an area of emphasis for the PhD as well. Two-thirds of the current graduate students take some advanced work in composition.

Maryland, College Park, offers an MA in rhetoric, linguistics, and pedagogy and allows students to take qualifying exams in composition and write dissertations in this field. Undergraduates can develop independent majors in composition.

At Nebraska, Lincoln, graduate students may take courses and an MA exam in composition and may use composition as a PhD area. This campus also offers a contract major, which may be developed in composition.

Iowa State offers MAs in technical writing, creative writing, and composition for the two-year community college. Prospective high school teachers can also focus on composition. Undergraduates at Iowa State may build individual concentrations in writing, linguistics, literature, or English education.

The English department at Michigan State offers a concentration in writing in its Emphasis 3 AB program, the general study of English literature and language.

Washington allows a BA minor in writing, creative or expository. Most students who choose this minor opt for creative writing, though recently some have minored in expository writing. A strong writers' program awards the MFA and features courses and workshops in poetry, fiction, and nonfiction prose.

From the variety of degree programs outlined here, many of them initiated or expanded in recent years, it is clear that composition is being increasingly treated as an appropriate field of graduate or undergraduate study. During the past ten years, research universities have begun offering their students more opportunities for writing and for studying writing, not only through degree programs and areas of concentration but also through cross-curricular efforts. These programs' principles and goals are commonly presented in written statements: while some of these may be simple handouts for new TAs, those I have seen are carefully articulated descriptions of the philosophies, structures, and procedures supporting the programs. They show how individual courses meet a program's aims and fit into the broader intellectual context offered by the history and study of rhetoric and composition. Recently, AAU writing programs have become both larger and more thoroughly informed by new and traditional understandings of the matter and practice of writing. Through graduate courses in rhetorical theory or the teaching of composition, as through innovative interdisciplinary programs influenced by current research, these programs are treating writing as a study—or an art—not only necessary but suitable for a research university.

CHAPTER 5

Faculty and Teaching Assistants

O F PARTICULAR INTEREST, as we examine the programs on AAU campuses during 1984-85, are the character, status, and training of the writing faculty. As writing programs have begun changing in scope and emphasis, the profiles of their instructors have begun changing as well. Indeed, because writing is still most often taught within or closely associated with English departments, most faculty members (ladder or temporary) and graduate assistants who teach writing have degrees in English or related fields. Some programs, however, given new administrative structures and wide responsibilities, now hire or assign faculty members from many other fields to teach writing.

Composition of the Faculty

The survey respondents identified their faculty members' fields as shown in table 32. The position of English and the rankings that follow are much what we would have expected. Under "Other" the field named most often was history. In three programs, the directors themselves hold PhDs in history (Jean Moss at Catholic, Charlene Sedgwick at Virginia, and Richard Marius at Harvard). At Michigan State, where freshman courses are taught in the Department of American Thought and Language, faculty members hold degrees in American studies and American history, as well as in fields listed above.

Some cross-curricular programs now depend on faculty members in fields widely removed from traditional areas of preparation. Campuses on which faculty members hold degrees in areas other than those listed include Carnegie-Mellon: computer science, philosophy, psychology; MIT: history of science, journalism, mechanical engineering, materials science, physics, linguistics, mathematics; and USC: cinema, religion, sociology, philosophy, history, economics, international relations, law, journalism, music, busi-

Table 32
In what fields do your faculty members hold degrees?

Field	Number of responses
English	41
Comparative literature	21
Creative writing	18
Linguistics	17
Rhetoric	12
Education	12
English as a second language	10
Speech	4
Communications	3
Other	9

Note: 41 responses.

Table 33
What academic ranks do your faculty members currently hold?

Academic rank	Number of responses
Teaching assistant or associate	33
Lecturer or instructor	
Part-time	24
Full-time	16
Assistant professor	29
Associate professor	29
Professor	26

Note: 43 responses.

ness, drama, German. (Since graduate students teach USC's writing classes, the fields mentioned are their current areas of study rather than the fields in which they hold degrees.)

At Vanderbilt, writing-intensive courses are taught not only in the English department but also in "a dozen other departments," including fine arts, history, philosophy, and political science (Scott Colley, letter to the author, 13 Dec. 1984). And at Clark, the writing-across-the curriculum program includes courses "in most departments."

The academic ranks of writing teachers in the programs studied are shown in table 33. In my conversations with directors and chairs, I learned about the distribution and assignments of the faculty members and TAs who teach writing courses. Predictably, there is a complete spread, from programs staffed entirely by TAs or lecturers through programs taught by "everybody you can imagine": tenured faculty members, first-year and advanced graduate students, part-time visiting instructors, and instructors on three-year appointments. At the far end of the scale are those programs in which only regular faculty members and TAs teach. The responses given during interviews indicate something of this spectrum of appointments.

Courses in the USC Freshman Writing Program are taught exclusively by graduate students, appointed as assistant lecturers. They come from various departments across campus. Of the 159 on the staff in 1984-85, 90 to 100 were from the humanities division (60 from English, others from linguistics and religion); but journalism, professional writing, and cinema also contributed "substantial contingents," ranging from 10 to 15.

At Minnesota, Minneapolis, writing courses are taught almost entirely by TAs, 75% from English language and literature, a large percentage from American studies, and some from history and education.

Iowa State's freshman writing courses, formerly taught by full-time faculty members, are now taught most often by adjuncts, 20 with three-year terminal appointments and 37 with annual appointments, and by the 30 TAs enrolled in the MA program.

At Oregon writing is taught by graduate teaching fellows and instructors, full- or part-time.

The UCLA writing program is staffed by 45 to 50 lecturers, recruited through national searches, and a nearly equal number of TAs.

In the English department at Michigan, freshman courses are taught primarily by TAs, and sophomore and junior courses are taught by faculty members and TAs. The English Composition Board hires lecturers for its work in assessment and tutoring; most of them teach at least one course outside the program as well (in the introductory composition program or in the residential colleges). Junior-year courses that emphasize writing are taught outside the ECB.

Most of Michigan State's freshman courses are taught by the American Thought and Language faculty. In that department, 25 to 30 temporary faculty members, nearly all of whom have PhDs, hold appointments as temporary assistant professors; 7 or 8 are hired for the year, the others term by term. Graduate students work only in the laboratory of the noncredit developmental program.

At Minnesota, St. Paul, writing is taught by 15 full-time tenured or tenure-track faculty members and by 7 or 8 TAs from other departments (English or American studies, for example), since there is no PhD program in rhetoric.

The Maryland, College Park, freshman courses are taught by 85 graduate students and the junior courses by 60 part-time faculty members and by 30 full-time faculty members who teach one section each.

At Pittsburgh, writing is taught by part-time and regular faculty members and by TAs. Between 30 and 40 part-time instructors teach no more than two courses a semester. Perhaps 15 of the faculty of 55 teach writing each year. And of the 65 TAs in the department, some 40 teach composition in any given semester.

Writing is taught at Purdue by regular faculty members (each expected to teach one service course a year), adjunct faculty members (28 to 30 in the fall, very few in the spring), and TAs.

At Indiana, Bloomington, writing is taught by 120 TAs and the 52-member English faculty. No part-time adjuncts are involved.

Carnegie-Mellon's freshman courses are taught by regular faculty and PhD candidates; two-thirds of the upper-division courses are taught by regular faculty, one-third by advanced graduate students. There are approximately 20 TAs each year.

At Catholic University, writing is taught by regular faculty members and by graduate students.

TAs teach most freshman writing courses at Washington University, although the director and some faculty members have taught them as well. A few adjuncts (6 or so) also teach regularly.

Virginia's required and intermediate writing courses are usually taught by graduate students, occasionally by faculty members or the director. The advanced course is taught by writers and journalists.

Freshman writing courses at Tulane are taught primarily by TAs; additional seminars are taught by regular faculty members.

TAs teach almost all the writing courses at Brown, but faculty members sometimes teach the introductory courses in poetry, fiction, and drama—viewed also as writing courses—and the course on special topics in writing. About 60 undergraduates work as peer tutors in the Brown University Writing Fellows Program.

The writing courses in Yale's English department are taught by regular faculty members or advanced graduate students; writing-intensive sections in various other disciplines are taught by graduate students in those disciplines. Tutorials in the residential dorms are offered by a staff of 12 professional tutors.

The number of writing courses faculty members and TAs teach every year varies, institution by institution. I do not have complete information on normal teaching loads, since some respondents interpreted "courses" in the question "How many courses do faculty members in each category [listed] teach during one academic year?" to mean "writing courses." Thus, responses for assistant professor, associate professor, and professor ranged between, on the one hand, four to six courses a year and, on the other, one or two. Notes like these were added: "Not all faculty teach comp. Assistant professors usually teach at least one course per year." "Writing only." The heaviest full loads reported for schools on the quarter system were seven and nine courses a year (at least one of these responses including summer), and on both campuses the teaching load was the same for assistant professors, associate professors, and professors. Similarly, the heaviest loads for those on the semester system were six courses a year, again the same for all three ranks.

In the categories of teaching assistant and lecturer (part- or full-time), responses varied as follows: on either the quarter or the semester system, most TAs teach one course or two; in two programs they teach three courses a term (though in one of these programs, the sections taught are not self-standing writing courses for which the graduate students hold full responsibility). Several said new TAs teach only one course a term, and two who indicated that their TAs teach two courses a term explained that class size is limited to twelve. Part-time lecturers may teach up to three courses a term, and full-time lecturers teach from one to four, the heaviest load being ten for the year, on a quarter system.

During interviews, respondents commented on the roles, attitudes, and assignments of teaching assistants, lecturers, and other faculty members in their programs. Some expressed regret and deep concern over the status of lecturers and the demands normally placed on them. One director, for example, described those holding temporary appointments in his program as professionals who are doing excellent work but who are "unknown to the faculty." Discussing TAs, some directors explained the difficulty and importance of managing training programs for such large groups, perhaps as many as one-third of them new each year. One director who felt that TAs in his program were overburdened said that it would take a great deal of money to create a better system. Faculty involvement in teaching writing was variously described: at one university there was until a few years ago "a mandarin distaste" for teaching writing; at another, faculty members are "very faithful" about this teaching. Thus, despite having various concerns about the status, preparation, and involvement of those teaching writing, directors clearly respect these people and are working to strengthen their positions.

Faculty Development and TA Training

Regardless of the particular mix of TAs, lecturers, and faculty members teaching writing, the issue of training and development is important in any writing program. Obviously, training graduate assistants to teach strengthens the program, at the same time preparing them for their own professional careers. Lecturers bring varieties of training and experience into a program: ideally, they should be asked to apply their knowledge to the problems of teaching writing, influencing the shape and direction of the program, and should also be encouraged to continue developing their skills and understanding. Further, they should come to know well the department and university they serve. Whether the faculty members involved are members of an English department or of other departments participating in a cross-curricular program, workshops or seminars may be a means of sharing information and strengthening the community. Table 34 shows some of the information on faculty development and TA training obtained through the questionnaire and interviews.

As we noted earlier, one of the most often cited areas of change in the past five years is graduate instruction. Many of the graduate courses in composition that have been developed are associated with TA-training programs. In addition, a number of faculty-development programs have been designed, either for temporary faculty members, to ensure the consistency and quality of instruction or to provide professional development for those who will return to the job market, or for regular faculty members, often in connection with a writing-across-the-curriculum program. Development programs for faculty members and TAs have received much attention and care in recent years. The following sections concern the various kinds described in interviews.

Table 34
What programs for faculty development are now in place?

Programs	Not applicable	Optional	Required
For TAs	3	4	35
For new faculty	5	12	7
For part-time faculty	7	7	6
For full-time, temporary faculty	8	4	4
For tenure-track faculty	9	8	1
For tenured faculty	9	8	1

Note: 42 responses.

Mentor Programs

At Purdue, Leonora Woodman uses a mentor system that she says she inherited, one that has been in use for fifteen years. New TAs attend a three-day orientation in the fall and then, during the term, attend weekly meetings of a two-hour colloquium. In the colloquium, they prepare for their work in the classroom, learn to grade papers, and, as time allows, study composition research. The mentors supervise paper grading and visit classes three times during the fall and twice in the spring.

On some campuses, major change has been identified with a faculty member who joined the staff and developed a more sophisticated TA-training program than had existed before. At Maryland, College Park, for example, a master-teacher system was introduced by Robert Coogan. Before Coogan came in 1973, the program had been run by graduate students. Eugene Hammond, Coogan's successor, says Coogan brought to the program "an intellectual interest in composition." He started training teachers and established the master-teacher program. Seven master teachers now work with approximately twenty-eight new TAs each year. The new TAs attend a one-week orientation, with master teachers making presentations; take a course during the fall semester; and meet in groups of four with master teachers. The master teachers, each given a one-course release, visit classes often and report their recommendations to the director, who begins visiting classes only in the second year.

Marilyn Sternglass explains that before Barry Kroll came to Indiana, Bloomington, TAs had a short workshop before the fall semester began and received classroom visits during the term. Kroll introduced an elective course for new TAs, and he and an assistant taught freshman composition and visited new TAs' classes. Then, during 1984-85, the training program was modified to include TA consultants: four graduate students were hired as consultants, each teaching a freshman class and working with four or five new TAs, visiting their classes and holding weekly meetings. The consultants are given released time, so that they teach one course rather than two each term. Though this plan is more expensive, the smaller nuclear groups offer valuable training and support.

Some program directors stress that TA training is now receiving attention. At Michigan, for example, the English department's Composition Program planned to introduce a new training program in 1985-86. The plan called for a forty-hour workshop in August to deal with the aims and goals of the freshman courses, teaching strategies, syllabus design, and paper grading. During the year, all new TAs would attend weekly seminars. Eight exceptional teachers (lecturers or fourth-year TAs) would serve as mentors, each working with four new TAs: they would work closely after the workshop, meeting weekly during the fall, visiting one another's classes, and being visited regularly by the mentors. The group of five would work "as a social unit, sharing problems and enthusiasms." This kind of support had been missing. The plan was proposed by Daniel Fader, and the dean provided funding for the mentors. For the lecturers, there would be no additional cost: though their teaching load is six courses a year, they are normally assigned five and allowed one-sixth time for supervision. To release three TAs from teaching during the fall term would cost $9,000.

Apprenticeships

Stanford has developed an apprenticeship program to prepare graduate students for teaching. Second-year graduate students take a pedagogy course in the fall and serve as apprentices to experienced instructors. Thus, they gain experience in grading and teaching classes before they begin teaching in the winter.

At Oregon, first-year graduate students serve apprenticeships to the director of composition. During the year, they attend a workshop, visit classes, and student-teach with other instructors. During their second year, they begin teaching composition. The difficulty is that they are not paid during the first year, and Oregon, John Gage says, loses some students to schools willing to give them immediate support. The program "creates enthusiasm in graduate students—and faculty support the program because they see what gets those students jobs: not just raw years, but quality of teaching." Recent graduate students with this training are finding academic positions.

Orientation, Courses, and Workshops

Most of the AAU universities studied seem now to have solid TA-training programs. Some say that these programs have recently become more formal. Most require a combination of course work, workshops, and supervision.

New TAs at Minnesota, Minneapolis, attend a ten-day workshop followed by weekly seminars with workshops, lectures, and group work. During the second and following years, they meet with faculty members in other disciplines to discuss and plan curricula. Donald Ross says that new TAs "leave their training sessions scared and eager—just about right."

Virginia begins its TA training in the spring: graduate students attend a two-day workshop, including separate meetings on commenting, choosing topics, classroom strategies, and grading. They also attend workshops during the semester.

TA training at Washington University has changed within the past two years in connection with changes in the content and structure of the freshman course. Graduate students become TAs in their second year: in their first semester as assistants, they teach one section of twelve students and take a training seminar with the director of freshman composition; in subsequent semesters, they teach two such sections and have staff meetings every two or three weeks, sometimes with faculty members from other disciplines. The training program also includes workshops and class observations. Most graduate students do teach, but appointments are no longer automatic: teaching "is a privilege awarded only after interviews and consideration of writing and grading samples."

At Penn, English 800 offers graduate-level instruction in literary fields while training new teaching assistants. The course is taught by two English faculty members. Both faculty members and TAs teach freshman courses, using material from the graduate seminar. The 800 course includes materials on teaching writing.

At Nebraska, Lincoln, beginning TAs take a graduate-level course in the theory of composition, as well as a one-credit course to accompany the course they are teaching. A sequence of composition-theory courses is required in almost all PhD programs.

At UCLA, students take a two-quarter practicum (with two units each quarter) during their first year of teaching, followed by a one-quarter (four-unit) course in composition theory, research, and pedagogy. This sequence reverses the former order; the change was made recently because students felt they were unprepared for theory and eager for practical advice during their first term in the classroom.

At Carnegie-Mellon, teaching is part of the doctoral program in rhetoric. TAs take a number of theoretical courses and participate in weekly workshops.

Programs for Tutors and Fellows

Schools that use tutors or fellows have developed training programs for them, again combining orientation, workshops, and seminars.

Writing fellows at Brown "are selected on the basis of both writing and counseling skills" (Brown University Writing Fellows Program, Nov. 1984). Applicants are required to submit three samples of their writing and are interviewed. In their first term, the fellows take a course in the teaching of writing. In this course, they learn peer tutoring and study the theory and practice of composition. They "practice their own writing . . . , as well as commenting on sample student papers." Their subsequent work is supervised by Tori Haring-Smith and by an experienced graduate student who works as the program's assistant director (Writing Fellows Program).

At Chicago, lectors for the Little Red Schoolhouse are selected on the basis of writing samples, comments on a student paper, and faculty recommendations. About one in six applicants is successful. The lectors attend a seminar on writing and language theory. They devote three weeks to the course itself (the Little Red Schoolhouse), four weeks to composition theory, and three weeks to classroom practice. Those who go on to become interns in the humanities core courses or dormitory tutors attend a three-day seminar followed by three or four group meetings.

Writing across the Curriculum

At Yale, graduate students who will teach writing-intensive sections attend five training sessions, two before classes begin and three follow-up sessions during the term. In these sessions, they deal with such tasks as making assignments, holding conferences, and commenting on drafts. Linda Peterson is "more than satisfied" with this program as a means of preparing students for their work in the program.

Similarly, in Penn's Writing across the University Program, senior fellows work directly with writing consultants in their areas, to supplement the training offered through orientation and workshops. Penn has also begun inviting affiliated faculty members to attend the workshops.

Faculty Development

The programs that hire large numbers of lecturers are also concerned with faculty development. At UCLA, for example, lecturers attend a three-day orientation late in the summer, participate in staff seminars, and serve on committees: in this way, they take responsibility for the program and also continue with their own professional development.

Some universities offer workshops for faculty members teaching in various departments. At Vanderbilt, Scott Colley, associate dean and chair of the Writing Committee, conducts the faculty workshops: he has worked with 80 of the 390 faculty members on campus. As Colley explains, he uses an informal method, gaining his colleagues' confidence and demonstrating how to save time in grading papers. Then, as someone who teaches writing, he "can rely on shared experienced." Three years after beginning these workshops, Colley finds the faculty very cooperative. When I spoke with him, he was planning a TA workshop for Christmas, a series of three one-day workshops, eight hours a day, for "Danish and $50." To that date, he had taught 150 TAs his method of grading.

Conferences

Because faculty members and teaching assistants may become involved in designing, planning, and presenting conferences hosted by their writing programs, conferences can be seen as another means of development and training. Within the past few years, the programs included in this study have held conferences focused on such topics as classical rhetoric and the teaching of writing, the politics of writing instruction, literacy, computers and writing, peer tutoring, and writing centers.

Hosting these conferences, AAU writing programs have shown an awareness of, and a sense of responsibility to, a national audience. The conferences serve members of the profession and local teachers, perhaps equally well. Because they provide a forum for exchanging information and for developing professional relationships, they become the occasion for faculty development. The writing programs studied are creating new, sometimes elaborate, means of supporting and training those who teach writing. Such efforts aim to increase the effectiveness of faculty members and teaching assistants, in English and in a variety of other fields, also giving them identity and status within the academic community.

CHAPTER 6

Attitudes, Opinions, and Plans

B ECAUSE A WRITING PROGRAM does not exist only within a table of
organization and statistical reports, I included survey questions on
such intangibles as attitudes, judgments, and predictions. I wanted to learn
from each director what place the program now holds in the university, how
difficult it is to change in each of its elements, and what might be expected of
it in coming years. Here, as in other sections of the survey, I looked to the
directors for informed opinions. Any program's welfare depends on political
as well as fiscal realities, on perceptions and loyalties as well as the quality of
teaching. Further, its stability rests on its capacity for change. While change
is not in and of itself a good, a program remains alive only if it can handle
and promote change. While change—positive or negative—can be imposed
from without, given such pressures as administrators' interests or financial
crises, it is also generated from within, as the director and faculty initiate or
respond to developments within the field, the campus, the program, or the
department. To estimate each program's status, effectiveness, and potential
for change, I included a set of questions on these topics. The answers are
shown in tables 35 to 40. Again, I have only fragments of information, which I
offer as opinion pieces. In these tables the columns headed NA give the number of respondents who found the items "not applicable," and those headed
NR, "no response," show the number who did not respond to the items.

Attitudes

In table 35 attitudes toward writing programs are reported to be quite
positive (predominantly rated 4 or 5) among four groups: the writing faculty,
campus administrators, writing program administrators, and graduate
students, though on three campuses graduate students' attitudes toward
the program are negative (rated 1 or 2). Attitudes are thought to be somewhat less positive among three other groups—undergraduate students, other
departments, and English departments—although ratings still cluster at
and above the midpoint of the scale. The ratings for English departments,

Table 35
On a scale of 1 (very negative) to 5 (very positive), how would you characterize the overall attitudes these groups or units show toward your writing program?

Group	Negative			Positive		NA	NR
	1	**2**	**3**	**4**	**5**	**NA**	**NR**
Undergraduate students	0	2	16	17	7	0	2
Graduate students	2	1	3	16	14	5	3
Writing faculty	0	1	4	19	15	1	4
Writing program administrators	2	0	3	16	14	5	4
English department	1	6	12	16	7	0	2
Home department (other than English)	0	0	1	0	5	19	19
Other departments	0	4	14	18	5	0	3
Campus administrators	0	2	7	21	12	0	2
Teachers or administrators in local schools	1	2	3	13	6	15	4

perhaps not surprisingly, vary more widely than those for any other group: 7 ratings of 5 and another 7 at the low end of the scale (6 ratings of 2 and a single rating of 1). Most of those programs not housed in English report positive attitudes in the home departments. Finally, the attitudes reported for teachers or administrators in the local schools are predominantly at the positive end, but 15 respondents found this category "not applicable" for their programs.

Degrees of Success

In rating how well writing programs serve various groups (see table 36), nearly all survey participants either found "home department (other than English)" not applicable or did not respond. Here, as on the preceding question, the large numbers in the NA and NR columns are not surprising, since indeed most programs are housed in English departments. Note, however, that the next largest number of not-applicable responses are for local schools. Many such responses are also given for Educational Opportunity Program (EOP) students and graduate students, and there are a sizable number for specially admitted students, juniors, seniors, and other departments. These responses remind us that the populations served by the programs studied vary widely: some universities do not have EOP programs, while others have large numbers of EOP students in their classes.

The single highest figure in table 36 is 25, the number of 4 ratings given for service to regularly admitted students. The next two highest scores, 23 and 21, are also 4 ratings, for service to freshmen and to the university. In each of these three categories, the next highest number of scores appears under the rating 5. All these groups are served well, in the opinion of the program directors.

Table 36
On a scale of 1 (very poorly) to 5 (very well), how would you rate the way your writing program serves each group or unit listed below? (These are overlapping classifications.)

Group	Poorly 1	2	3	Well 4	5	NA	NR
Regularly admitted students	0	1	5	25	11	0	2
Specially admitted students	3	5	10	9	5	9	3
Honors students	1	4	8	13	12	3	3
Educational Opportunity Program students	2	2	8	10	2	14	6
Second-language students	5	9	13	8	5	2	2
Transfer students	2	2	11	18	6	2	3
Freshmen	0	1	7	23	10	0	3
Sophomores	1	3	11	16	3	5	5
Juniors	1	5	4	19	4	8	3
Seniors	2	5	5	12	8	8	4
Graduate students	2	4	6	9	6	13	4
English department	1	2	4	17	13	4	3
Home department (other than English)	0	1	1	4	0	22	16
Other departments	0	3	8	20	3	7	3
University	1	0	9	21	10	0	3
Local schools	4	2	6	6	3	17	6

A considerable number of 4 ratings were also given for other departments (20), juniors (19), transfer students (18), English departments (17), and sophomores (16). With the exception of English departments, which are thought to be served quite well, these groups are seen as somewhat less uniformly well served.

Because responses begin to even out below 16, we might look at the two highest scores for each remaining group. Here, honors students score highest, with seniors next. The groups remaining are specially admitted students, EOP students, and second-language students, together with graduate students and local schools. These groups receive not only the lowest scores overall but also, as we have seen, a large number of not-applicable responses.

Programmatic and Curricular Change

Survey participants were asked to use a scale of 1 (very difficult) to 5 (very easy) to rank the difficulty of making various kinds of changes in their programs. Tables 37 to 40 report their responses. On the question of modifying or creating courses and programs (table 37), the replies indicate, as we might expect, that it is easier to modify than to create either courses or programs and easier to change courses than to change programs. But the highest num-

Table 37
Difficulty of Changing Courses and Programs

| | Difficult | | | Easy | | | |
Type of change	1	2	3	4	5	NA	NR
Modify existing courses	5	3	11	6	16	0	3
Create new courses	8	5	15	7	5	0	4
Modify existing programs	9	5	12	6	6	0	6
Create new programs	12	8	13	1	4	1	5

Table 38
Difficulty of Changing Requirements and Tests

| | Difficult | | | Easy | | | |
Type of change	1	2	3	4	5	NA	NR
Change writing requirements	22	7	9	0	3	0	3
Modify existing writing tests	3	1	9	7	6	13	5

ber of responses (16), from those considering it very easy to modify existing courses, is not matched by the number judging it very difficult to create new programs (12). There is a greater spread in responses to these items than we might have anticipated. For 11 to 15 respondents it is neither especially easy nor especially difficult to make any of these changes. And 5 find it difficult to modify existing courses, while 4 find it easy to introduce new programs. This set of responses again demonstrates the variousness of programs and of their circumstances.

Table 38 shows how respondents viewed the difficulty of changing writing requirements and exams. They found requirements extremely difficult to change: the number of 1 ratings (22) is the highest in tables 36 to 39, in contrast to the few 5 ratings on this item (3). Perhaps because a number of schools do not administer writing tests, 13 respondents indicated that the item on modifying writing tests is inapplicable. The 26 who did reply estimated varying degrees of difficulty in changing tests.

On the question of hiring faculty members (table 39), the responses of "not applicable" are perhaps as interesting as the judgments of difficulty. Sizable numbers indicated that the question did not apply for full-time, temporary faculty (17), part-time faculty (14), and full-time, tenure-track faculty (12). While the figures here confirm overwhelmingly that indeed tenure-track appointments are the most difficult, if not impossible, to make, they also show that temporary appointments are not uniformly made and that full-time temporary appointments are not often made easily.

Regarding the difficulty of various other program changes (table 40), the responses are often more evenly distributed than those in table 39. Note-

Table 39
Difficulty of Hiring Faculty Members

Faculty category	Difficult			Easy		NA	NR
	1	2	3	4	5		
Graduate students	2	2	6	10	14	6	4
Part-time faculty	2	3	8	8	6	14	3
Full-time, temporary faculty	5	6	2	5	3	17	6
Full-time, tenure-track faculty	17	3	4	1	0	12	7

Table 40
Difficulty of Miscellaneous Program Changes

Type of change	Difficult			Easy		NA	NR
	1	2	3	4	5		
Work with faculty in other departments	2	8	10	11	6	2	5
Introduce faculty-development programs	7	9	11	5	2	3	7
Arrange released time for faculty	12	8	5	2	2	9	6
Make administrative appointments	11	7	4	3	2	11	6
Change your program's administrative structure	6	10	7	5	5	6	5
Develop programs for local schools	6	4	9	3	5	12	5
Develop joint projects with other postsecondary institutions							
In the area	5	6	9	5	3	12	4
In the state	5	8	7	4	3	13	4
In organizations to which your institution belongs	5	6	6	6	3	14	4

worthy here are the many who replied "not applicable" to cooperative projects, with local schools or with other postsecondary institutions. Similarly, a good number of respondents said that the question about making new administrative appointments did not apply. Fewer found the next question, on changing the program's administrative structure, inapplicable, and there is an unusually wide spread of opinion about the difficulty of making such changes.

Table 41
Are you making or planning to make major changes in your program?

Response	Number of responses
Yes	17
No	20
Maybe	1
Yes, graduate; no, undergraduate	1

Note: 39 responses.

Plans for Change

Table 41 shows how many survey participants are planning major changes in their programs. If "maybe" and "yes, at the graduate level" are treated as positive responses, the *yes*es (19) nearly equal the *no*es (20). In contrast, more than four times as many said yes (36) as no (8) to the earlier question about whether there had been major changes during the past ten years. Of the 8 reporting no major changes in that period, 4 said they are now making or planning changes and 2 said they are not; another 2 did not respond to the question. Of the 36 who said that their programs had already changed, 15 expect more changes and 18 do not, while 3 did not respond to the question. (See the discussion of responses to the first survey question, in chapter 1.) These figures suggest that most of the 44 programs studied have already gone through what may be their most dramatic changes for some time. During interviews, however, I sensed that the programs described to me will not remain static but will continue developing to meet their students' needs in what are found to be the most effective ways.

Table 42 identifies the areas in which survey participants expect to make changes in their programs. The area with by far the largest number of responses is computer programs: 15 participants expect changes in the type of computer programs they are using, and 22 expect the number to increase. All other items can be divided into two groups, those with scores of 1 to 6 and those with 7 to 12. (Note that in table 4, which shows changes made over the past five years, scores fall predominantly between 10 and 20; we can infer that more programs have experienced change than are now anticipating change.) The group with scores of 7 to 12 includes graduate and advanced courses, campuswide requirements, and faculty positions—all expected to change in type and increase in number. Also in this group are introductory and intermediate courses and workshops, expected to increase in number.

Table 42
Within the next five years, in which areas do you expect change?

Area of change	Type		Number	
	New	**Change**	**Increase**	**Decrease**
Courses, programs, or services				
Preparatory	0	4	5	0
Introductory	0	6	9	0
Intermediate	0	4	9	0
Advanced	0	7	10	0
Graduate	2	10	12	0
Faculty	0	5	5	0
Schools	0	3	3	0
Other: adjunct, coregistered	1	0	0	0
Positions				
Administrative	0	3	6	0
Faculty	2	10	10	1
Clerical	0	4	4	0
Requirements				
Campuswide	1	10	8	0
Divisional	0	1	1	0
Departmental	0	4	4	1
Examinations	0	1	2	2
Instruction				
Courses	0	3	4	0
Seminars	1	2	2	0
Workshops	0	4	7	0
Tutorials	0	4	6	0
Students enrolled or participating				
For credit	0	5	8	3
For no credit	0	2	4	0
Support services	1	5	6	0
Additional resources				
Computer programs	3	15	22	0
Videotapes	0	1	2	0
Television programs	0	0	0	0
Audio programs	0	0	0	0
Other self-paced learning materials	1	2	3	0
Other: word processors	1	1	1	0

Note: 36 responses.

Finally, respondents expect more students to enroll for credit. If we look only at the highest rankings in the group with scores of 1 to 6, we see that increases are also expected in support services, tutorials, and administrative positions. Some directors expect changes in the other areas listed, but very few expect decreasing numbers in any area.

Table 43
Within the next five years, how do you
expect your budget to change?

Response	Number of responses
Marked increase	7
Slight increase	23
No change	6
Slight decrease	3
Marked decrease	0

Note: 39 responses.

Table 44
Funding: Comparison of Projections and Reported Changes

	Changes over the past five years				
Projections	Marked increase	Slight increase	No change	Slight decrease	Marked decrease
Marked increase	6	1	0	0	0
Slight increase	8	13	1	1	0
No change	1	2	2	1	0
Slight decrease	1	1	0	1	0
Marked decrease	0	0	0	0	0

Projections on Funding

The budget projections tabulated in table 43 can be usefully compared with reports on previous budgets. The responses given in this table are broken down in table 44 according to budgetary changes reported for the past five years (shown above in table 4). This analysis shows, for example, that of the 7 now expecting marked increases, 6 received marked increases over the past five years and 1 received a slight increase during that time.

Nearly all those expecting marked increases have already seen their budgets increase substantially. Similarly, nearly all anticipating slight increases have already received some increase (slight or marked) over the past five years. The 2 that did not had earlier received substantial funding. Some in this category, anticipating slight increases, expect an increase only to cover cost-of-living expenses, and 1 noted that change depends on the general economy. Of those expecting no change or a slight decrease, only 2 do not expect their funding in five years to match or exceed that of five years ago: 1, after experiencing a slight decrease, now expects no change, and the other expects a second slight decrease. Of these 39 programs, then, only 2 are expected to show financial declines over the periods of time studied (1979-84, 1984-89).

Clearly, most directors expect to hold the ground they have gained during the past five years. They expect their programs to continue doing well, given the resources and support already earned. Of course, these directors can identify the weaknesses of their programs as well as the strengths, and they know the difficulties of working in a field still questioned by some of their peers. Even so, the 1984-85 reports on the 44 programs studied are remarkably positive: these programs have changed substantially, and they show promise of continuing health. Perhaps their long-term viability will depend on how well they have secured their positions on campus and, more broadly, on what status they are attaining within the academy.

CHAPTER 7

English and Composition

THE WRITING PROGRAMS described to me in 1984-85 have changed dramatically over the years, particularly since the late seventies, and they will continue making readjustments. Though some are only now hiring new directors, commissioned to give the programs renewed coherence and purpose, most already have the identity and direction they expect to maintain. These programs do not all fit squarely within traditional university structures, however, and their continuing stability depends on political and intellectual forces their directors recognize very well.

Because my information has come from program directors, I turn to them for insight into the status and prospects of these programs. I have reported some of their attitudes and opinions statistically, but two issues remain: What kind of rapport do writing programs now have with English departments? And do directors themselves consider composition an academic discipline?

We have already considered structural relations between writing programs and the English departments that still house or support them. We have thought, too, about the issues of tenure and promotion. And we very early assessed the importance of departmental support for program changes. Though I repeat here some of the details and themes presented earlier, I want now to show the full spectrum of attitudes and relations described to me.

Let me say first that I have heard tales of anger, frustration, and distress. When one program separated from the English department, English faculty members were angry, primarily because of "the timing and the insult." "The lecturers who staff our writing program do feel like second-class citizens, unwelcome in the English department." "The TAs have been angry because they're not paid well here. And when they go on the market, they don't get jobs." "Composition's status is not an issue on our campus—because it has no status."

But usually more is said. "Some would consider these [writing program activities] janitorial services," but they respect the director's work in literary criticism and linguistics, and they admire his political sense. Further, faculty members cannot easily dismiss a program that gives their graduate students substantial training and financial aid. In one department, "a small, vocal, powerful, and increasingly bitter minority opposed [changes in the program] at every step. . . . They felt disenfranchised. But they are now quiet and resigned." "They respect our program because it's research-based." "Lecturers leaving our program are getting tenure-track jobs in literature, composition, or both."

As I looked over my interview notes and began to outline the responses to questions about relations with English departments, I found more optimism and positive signs than I would have expected before I began this study—never blind optimism, and few clear and final victories, but often a sense of achievement and definite evidence of gain. Let me outline some of my findings.

At one university, there was some division, some question of whether to hire a composition specialist or a literary scholar interested in composition. The person selected, finally, was a literary scholar, one who's directing what sounds like a creative, solid program. The department prides itself on having chosen unity. Yet it will have to advance a tenure recommendation to the dean. The director expects his administrative work to be credited as high-grade departmental service.

At Iowa State, the balance between literature and composition has shifted in the past decade. The university itself has seen unusual growth in certain areas: a college of business was recently formed, for example. The dramatic expansion of technical- and business-writing courses "has almost set a direction for the department."

Language, writing, and rhetoric, a field in the English department at Tulane, is seen as an important resource for graduate students. The division was created recently and a faculty of three hired. Though none of them has yet come up for tenure, the department is very supportive.

Both Oregon and Nebraska, Lincoln, have long traditions of teaching and valuing composition in their English departments. Project English started at Oregon, and Albert Kitzhaber only recently retired from the department. Dudley Bailey chaired the English department at Nebraska, Lincoln, and he was honored on retirement with a conference on the politics of writing instruction.

Tapping into the rhetorical tradition, a number of schools offer degrees in rhetoric or rhetoric and composition: these include Minnesota, St. Paul, where the Department of Rhetoric has undergraduate and master's degrees in technical communication; Catholic University, which recently hosted a conference on classical rhetoric and the teaching of writing and is now planning a graduate program; and Purdue, which created a graduate program in 1981.

Many directors have devoted research and teaching to composition and its relation to literary studies. Several credited their colleagues with earning respect for composition and their programs, and some confirmed that scholarship in rhetoric and composition is valued in decisions on promotion and tenure. Eugene Hammond explained, for example, that the English department at Maryland, College Park, has resolved that in tenure decisions composition shall have as much weight as any other field. A number of directors mentioned that their graduate students are doing unusually well at finding academic appointments after receiving their degrees.

Though, overall, relationships between writing programs and English departments are still considered unequal, writing does hold a secure position on certain campuses. Carnegie-Mellon, for example, has undergone what Gary Waller describes as "a double revolution," the revolution in composition preceding and now starting to interact with that in literary and cultural studies. Two responses I received to a question about composition's status on campus are especially pertinent. At one university, faculty members teaching literature feel that the writing enterprise receives too much money. "They're also jealous of [its] status," though this issue "is not subject for much discussion." Even there, people in writing sometimes "don't get as much honor as we think due . . . but I think that's the state of the academic mind generally." At another university, the director would like to say that composition's status is not an issue at all—"but there's still an undercurrent of anger and nervousness because composition is where all the action is, and all the energy."

With the strength and favor of writing programs ranging between extremes, we might expect their directors to have widely varying perspectives on "composition." I asked them in interviews, "Do you consider composition an independent scholarly discipline?" Because the answers veer away from classifications, a tally is less important than the language, the lines of reasoning, and the spectrum of response: these show as much about the state of composition as do the numbers.

Typically, directors who answered yes to this question feel that composition deserves independent status because of its increasing sophistication and professionalism. It now has its own journals, graduate programs, organizations, and conferences. One response was, "Yes. It seems to me that within English departments there has been tension, but it's clearly settled, given the extent and quality of research in recent years—and the political realities. . . . We have separation, whether or not it's totally desirable." Is it a discipline? "Yes, it is. And that may be a problem. . . . It's independent before it's welcome, so structurally it's not independent on many campuses. It's not recognized by the mother—no, the father—department. It's a discipline in search of recognition." (This comment was made by the director of a program not included in this study; I repeat it here because it characterizes well the attitude expressed in several interviews.)

Other directors present the counterargument that composition is not a discipline or that it has gone about achieving separation in the wrong way. One said, when asked whether composition is an independent scholarly discipline, "I suppose not. That's a hard question. Yes and no—which helps you not at all. The word *scholarly* is what brings me up short. It's getting more complex, dealing with the theory of learning and joining up with modern criticism. But I have trouble with deconstructive theories of composition." Another response: "My perception . . . is that, to a great extent, the profession of composition has taken a wrong direction. A lot of what proclaims itself as research is fundamentally misconceived." The same respondent described some of what he sees in the journals as "deliberate false naïveté," giving as an example the discovery that after all these years we know little about the process of reading. He added that "the general activity in recent years has been helpful, but the specific activity has been questionable."

Another director, granting that research has probably given composition credence as a discipline, admitted that personally she doesn't value empirical research in writing. She, like others, much prefers the work now being done on the history of rhetoric. Yet linking composition with rhetoric does not settle the issue of composition's status. Note, for example, this paired set of responses to the question "Is composition a discipline?" The first is a firm and immediate yes: "Composition and rhetoric. It's the most ancient and respectable of all the humanistic disciplines. Of course, I was trained as a medievalist. I see it as a perfectly legitimate field of academic endeavor." The second response is no: "I came to [composition] from rhetoric, so it doesn't seem independent to me." Both these directors, however, emphasized rhetoric's connection with literature and concluded that composition does not need to become a separate department. Thus, answers of yes and no may have similar sources and lead toward similar conclusions.

Many directors advocate maintaining and strengthening associations with English departments. They argue, in fact, that compartmentalization could be destructive and that a new relationship should be established. Those who see rhetoric as the means of redefining the relationship emphasize the scope of this field: "Rhetoric can draw on psychology and educational theory as well as on historical and contemporary rhetorical theory. It's an all-encompassing discipline that explains the procedures for interpreting literature. It's broader than literature." Others echo this affirmation of varied interests and resources: "I think, in fact, that if we could build the relationship between literary theory, reading theory, learning theory, psycholinguistics, and composition, that would go a long way toward making English departments primarily interested in literature think we're talking about common issues."

Finally, some directors and chairs commented on the concept of a discipline and on the means of deciding composition's place in the academy. They made these observations:

> My response, personally, would be that anything is an independent discipline if enough people are interested in it. Whether it is wise philosophically, pedagogically, and pragmatically [to view composition as a separate discipline] is another matter. I would hate to see composition taken out of the department. That would be impoverishing for both

sides. My department should be called a Department of Discourse Studies, but, of course, you have to work within existing labels.

It depends on how you define composition. I consider it a subset of discourse studies, which include linguistics, language, discourse analysis, and rhetoric. I suppose it would be called rhetoric. It is the local problem of teaching people how to engage in discourse. . . . A number of faculty members are now talking about setting up a committee on discourse, a committee including people from education, anthropology, English, and linguistics.

I think of it as an interdisciplinary study—or perhaps such a synthetic study that it reaches out and steals from everybody.

These three responses, particularly in the context of responses cited earlier, highlight the problems in defining composition as a discipline and the political realities that bear on any such definition. Composition is not self-contained, either in its practice or in the theories that explain and support it. It cannot, then, be defined simply in its own terms. Perhaps composition is best described as frankly acquisitive, a discipline borrowing from others, even as it serves them: composition is a means of communicating and developing what is central to other disciplines, and it in turn depends on their resources and needs.

This argument underlies one extended response to the question "Do you consider composition an independent scholarly discipline?"

No. The worst thing that has happened to composition is that it has begun to think of itself as an independent scholarly discipline, even though its methods and procedures are inchoate and untested. . . . Composition is still searching for its key methods and key texts. There's been one . . . sidetrack into cognitive psychology, treating writing as behavior. [This type of study] could highlight problems we hadn't seen before. But we have given away interpretation, the history of culture, influence—the most interesting things in composition. . . . Of course, composition is always reactive. The metaphors are always inadequate. The worst thing is that some have decided it is a discipline with its own tradition and its own center. It will not have a center. We can't describe writing because we can't find it. This is what makes the study of composition so interesting.

We need better journals. And we need to encourage more people in other disciplines (including English) to look at student writing and student reading. We need those who look at the structures of disciplines to look at them as they are represented by or to freshmen and sophomores. We need to interest them more, not in our research, but in the thing we're studying. There is no genre yet. The articles published never quote more than a few lines of student writing. We need longer, more serious, more speculative pieces. . . . Our generation should turn against the division of the generation before us: literature and composition, MLA and CCCC.

Looking in the other direction has meant only appeasement or humilia-
tion. Those in composition have made a virtue of isolation. We need to
imagine ourselves part of an intellectual community as other academics do.

We need to interest others in writing, "the thing we're studying" ("I consider
it a subset of discourse studies"), and we need the help of those "who look at
the structures of disciplines."

Because composition is a "discipline" that calls into question the notion of
discipline and because it has not yet found a natural home, it seems that
writing programs will continue struggling with questions of identity and
status. We have seen that most programs remain in or near English
departments, while some are moving toward greater independence. As
tempting as it might be to find a solution by taking a single program as a
model and pronouncing it best, such a solution could finally only weaken the
position of other programs across the country: those that work well but do
not fit the model would be declared, from within the profession, to be inadequate or at least second best, and those that tried to emulate the new model
but found it unworkable on other campuses would suffer as well.

If recognized leaders in the field argue here, as at our conferences and in
our journals, that composition is many things—a new discipline, an old discipline, a nondiscipline—should we not expect to find writing programs of
many stripes being developed and, with good fortune, succeeding on campuses of different characters and sizes? Further, if composition depends not
only on theories and opinions about it but also on its incarnations in writing
programs, should we not expect to find its reality governed—or at least profoundly influenced—by the particulars of its many situations? As the opening pages of this report indicate, the elements of change identified by program directors include everything from support by the administration and
the department chair to timing and circumstance—and I added a final
category, unnamed by the directors but obvious to me from my conversations with them: their own leadership in determining what would work, in
knowing when to take risks and when to show restraint. The character and
vitality of this discipline, which traces its sources to the classical age and yet
lays claim to becoming a new thing, will continue to depend fundamentally
on such practical realities as politics, finances, and personalities. Because
the battles joined, the issues addressed will be dictated by exigencies
perhaps as much as by principles, we must continue to monitor developments on individual campuses across the country.

We have seen, in the course of this study, that writing is being treated with
new—or renewed—seriousness on the campuses of major research universities. We have seen that degree programs are being developed or strengthened and that some faculty members are earning promotion and tenure for
their work in composition. What we have not seen, however, is any unanim-

ity about the form and ultimate value of work in this field. (One director commented that composition won't be established as a legitimate academic discipline until someone in the field earns tenure in the Ivy League. Another pointed out that such tenure decisions will be made soon.)

The writing program directors on AAU campuses strongly disagree about whether or not composition is or should seek to become "an independent scholarly discipline," and some believe that one way of resolving the problem is to open the discipline to other areas, to define it as a synthetic field of study, an interdisciplinary activity. The assumption here is that, since writing is practiced in all fields, its students and scholars can use the insights, the research, even—if they want—the vocabularies of those fields. At a time when disciplines are themselves changing and intertwining, writing poses a problem fundamental to our understanding of academic processes and structures: given that writing is needed for critical inquiry, how do students learn to write, who should study and teach writing, and what kinds of programs or administrative strategies will allow this research, teaching, and learning to occur? Restated, the problem is this: who holds and can exercise authority in this field?

The problem of authority has these, among other, manifestations: faculties disagree about whether or not writing courses are somehow as weighty as other university courses, about whether or not writing courses should be taught by apprentice and temporary faculty members, about whether or not writing deserves and can sustain scholarly investigation, and about whether writing programs exist at the center or at the periphery of the academic enterprise. Writing, amorphous as it is, can be seen as some kind of intellectual prop or as an engine of critical inquiry. In recent years, writing has gained in professional respectability, and, as it has done so, its proponents have begun making claims for their own authority. They want the power to define their subject and their territory, and they want status equal to that of other academics.

One difficulty has been that the writing camp is itself divided: some identify writing as a field within English studies (therefore properly placed inside English departments); others emphasize writing's rhetorical heritage (leading perhaps toward a solid and broadly defined program of communication studies); still others stress writing's uniqueness and its interdisciplinary status (suggesting new or at least unusual administrative structures). How can authority be gained in each case? In the first, by making writing equivalent to other fields represented in English departments: eighteenth-century literature, drama, modern American literature. In the second, by making it equivalent to other departments or interdisciplinary programs: the English department, the physics department, a center for medieval and Renaissance studies (assuming that center has a charter for teaching as well as for research). In the third, perhaps by equivalence with other interdisciplinary programs or perhaps through administrative intervention, some combination of resources, reputation, and support that will allow the program life. But if all three efforts go ahead at the same time, none of them will in itself finally give writing academic legitimacy.

The difficulty lies in the attempt to generalize, to reach beyond the campus (where any of these programs might work very well) to the profession. "The profession," of course, still commonly refers to that of English professors, and here we come upon a continuing power struggle, writing teachers—often themselves established English professors—seeking new recognition within or outside this profession. If the attempt is to establish writing as an acceptable academic field, the counsel to stay in or leave the English department probably has less value than does the excellence of a performance given on either stage. Very simply, the greater power still resides in English—and other—departments. Writing is gaining strength for many reasons, among them the quality of teaching, the increase in research and publication, and the new vitality of leadership in the field. Even so, this field does not yet have the strength or the security that inheres in a more solid component of the academic establishment. While it is important to keep imagining how this "profession" should be shaped and to keep professing faith in it, it now seems equally important to continue developing writing programs that work. In the coalitions, the agreements, and the joint projects developed on individual campuses, we can assess the validity of our projections about this profession.

As long as there is uncertainty about what composition is, the question of what place it holds on campus—and in the academy—will remain central. Because composition seems such an unusual field, unusual arrangements are being made for it. But notice that its position is still most often defined by its relation to an English department: a writing program ordinarily exists somewhere in, near, or outside an English department. Historically and pragmatically, there's very good reason for this reference to the English department: writing programs have been related to English departments, and we understand what English departments are. A writing program seems to have stature insofar as it is like, or as good as, an English department. Given some recent administrative experiments, we might look beyond the English department to other departments or programs, as I've suggested, but still we're looking to normal academic structures for reassuring comparisons. And these comparisons don't always work.

What does writing (or rhetoric and composition) do? It "reaches out and steals from everybody." It absorbs the strategies, wisdom, and language of other departments, and it serves them in turn. Math is commonly used outside the math department, but no one seems to worry about math's losing its identity. What happens then with writing? It seems to turn inside out, to become something it wasn't, even to disappear. What kind of discipline is as slippery as this? Why are so many people spending so much time trying to explain what it is—and to dignify it within the academy? And why are so many people working so hard to set up writing programs that fit the idiosyncratic needs of their own campuses? Given all that I have seen and heard of these programs, I would say that many of them are trying to become something they are not: familiar academic units that cause little trouble. Ironically, that's just what they used to be, harmless and unobtrusive freshman writing programs that simply ticked over from year to year, generally without notice. Now they cause notice. Now, in trying to become respectable and vigorous citizens of the academy, they're threatening to upset common notions of citizenship. If they can't slip quietly into position as normal departments, maybe they shouldn't try to do so.

Writing programs may not be doing something wrong then they fail to be recognized as proper academic units: they may in fact bring into question our common understanding of academic structures and procedures, our very notion of academic legitimacy. I wish I could foretell what will result from this kind of questioning, perhaps new interdisciplinary programs with new lines of responsibility. But it's not clear how much change is possible, how soon. Our universities are constructed around departments, and full professors earn more money and more respect than temporary lecturers. But writing programs are forcing us to see again how restrictive some of our normal practices can be. Instead of predicting, then, how things should finally turn out, I want to repeat that the options being tried, the questions being asked, are in and of themselves important.

For writing programs, this is a time of testing and of change, a time of growth. What matters in the portrait I've presented is not just the lines and dimensions of single programs or of all of them together but also the fact of their change over time. For this reason, I've tried to set them in their own historical contexts, showing something of what they have been and what they may become. In effecting change, these programs have both depended on and pushed against academic traditions. As a result, though the programs have themselves been transformed, many of them still rest uneasily within the academy, and in that very uneasiness, I would argue, lies strength. Integrating these programs into the academic life of their campuses, like integrating writing into the curriculum, requires an understanding of how the university works. It may also require a certain kind of courage. Maybe these programs will remain viable only as long as they continue to change in response to developments on campus and in the profession. Maybe they will remain valuable only as long as they call academic traditions and practices into question.

PART TWO

Case Studies

Introduction

IN THE COMPOSITE OF WRITING programs presented in the first half of this report, we have seen the elements and the variousness of 44 different programs. We turn now to a description and an analysis of three individual programs, varying in their elements and in their design. In the spring of 1985 I visited Harvard, Penn, and North Carolina, Chapel Hill, speaking with faculty members and administrators and reading items from the files. (An agenda and a list of materials reviewed follow each of the case studies below.) I could have chosen any of the programs for closer study, and I'm sorry that I have had to limit my time and attention to three. Let me explain my choices.

The writing program at the University of North Carolina, Chapel Hill, is housed in the English department and directed by Erika Lindemann, an associate professor hired and tenured for her work in composition. With a staff of about a hundred TAs, twenty-five to thirty of them new each year, this large program depends on a strong TA-training program—and a strong director—for continuity. In addition, faculty members are regularly involved in teaching and supervising writing courses, demonstrating and strengthening the program's fit within the department. The program and its director are respected within the university, and they suit that university well.

The University of Pennsylvania has two writing programs, separate but joined by their placement within the English department. Writing across the University (WATU), an innovative program established in 1982, employs graduate students from a variety of disciplines as writing fellows. The fellows work as teaching assistants or consultants to emphasize writing in courses taught across campus. At the time of the survey, 1984-85, Peshe Kuriloff was in her first year as coordinator of WATU and its affiliated Writing Center. Holding an annual appointment, she teaches half time in addition to administering the program. Holding a similar appointment, David Espey coordinates the freshman English seminars and graduate studies. In this position, he manages a large, elective program, part of Penn's Freshman Seminar Program, and he helps graduate students maintain connections between their study and teaching. Both programs fit well with the philosophy and traditions of this university.

The strong and independent Expository Writing Program at Harvard University is under the direction of Richard Marius. A historian, novelist, and journalist, Marius is a senior lecturer in expository writing. He has given this program its character, both because he is its primary link to the university and because he has hired a faculty of writers. Though they hold temporary appointments, many have continued in the program for a number of years. These experienced preceptors have assumed a role in administering the program and in shaping its courses.

These three examples, then, represent some of the variety we now see in writing programs. They differ in leadership, administrative structure, staffing, curriculum, and purpose; yet they all suit their campuses precisely. We see them in different stages of evolution, and we see them in the process of change. Here, in fact, we find the vitality characterizing each of these programs. As a result, studying them as they were in one academic year, 1984-85, we will see not only their individual administrative designs, but also their patterns of change.

CHAPTER 8

The University of North Carolina, Chapel Hill

A STUDY OF THE WRITING program at the University of North Carolina, Chapel Hill, is a study of change from within. In five years as director of composition, Erika Lindemann has given the program new strength and coherence. She has done so by working within existing structures: accepting the courses, administrative structures, and traditions she inherited, she has tested and strengthened each of them. She has not imposed change but, rather, encouraged it, allowing it to occur. She has not acted singly or arbitrarily but, rather, has shared her authority and her knowledge so that change has occurred naturally, almost inevitably. Lindemann's strategy has been especially fitting for this program, given its place in the university.

The distinctive character of the university is suggested in two recent self-studies, the first focused on the undergraduate curriculum, the second on the research mission of the university. These reviews deserve our notice because they display Chapel Hill's careful balance between tradition and reform and because they help place the writing program in its university context.

From 1979 to 1981, more than two hundred faculty members were involved in thoroughly reexamining the undergraduate curriculum. This study, initiated by Samuel R. Williamson, Jr., the dean of the College of Arts and Sciences, resulted in a new curriculum, unanimously approved by the Faculty Council. This curriculum reflects the faculty's understanding of undergraduate education. Students now move through a sequence of three types of courses: basic skills, perspectives, and capstone. Basic skills include composition and reading, foreign languages, and mathematics. Perspectives are "approaches to knowledge" that give students "a sense of perspective regarding the world in which [we live] and the characteristic approaches to knowledge which shape [an] understanding of it . . . " (quoted in the final report of the 1984 Task Group X: The Quality of Undergraduate Education Appropriate to a Research University 30). Students are exposed to these six perspectives on knowledge: natural science, aesthetic, Western historical, non-Western comparative, social science, and philosophical. Capstone courses "take a wholistic look at some subjects—to approach them through an awareness of their assumptions and their potentialities and implications for human welfare" (quoted in Quality of Undergraduate Education 31).

In addressing the basic skills, the faculty reaffirmed the two-semester composition requirement, described to me by Stephen Birdsall, acting dean of the College of Arts and Sciences, as the only program in the college that has always been mandatory. Further, the faculty indirectly affirmed the importance of writing in upper-division courses. William Graves, holding the new position of associate dean for general education, offered this explanation: The general-education requirements are no longer confined to the first two years; students must now take five perspectives during their junior and senior years. Courses proposed for the perspectives category must maintain small sections, require in-depth study resulting in a project (most often a paper), and give evidence that writing will be carefully reviewed. This Graves explains as "a back-door approach to writing across the curriculum," an approach that will work at Chapel Hill.

More recently, in a self-study for reaccreditation by the Southern Association of Colleges and Schools, the university reexamined its research mission. One task group was assigned to describe and assess the quality of undergraduate education and to recommend improvements consistent with that research mission. In its final report (cited above), the task group pointed out that since 1795 the university has emphasized teaching as well as research. The task group rigorously assessed the implications of this dual commitment, viewing research and teaching as "complementary activities that interact to sustain [a] vigorous intellectual climate" (15-16) and treating quality education as the shared responsibility "of all who participate in the life of the University" (19). The task group offered twenty-five recommendations, addressed variously to students, committees, and administrative officers. These recommendations showed concern about excellence and innovation in teaching and about the roles of faculty members and graduate students in undergraduate instruction. Throughout its report, the task group advocated means of enhancing the "vital intellectual atmosphere" appropriate to a research university with a faculty of "scholar-teachers" (7).

As these two self-studies suggest, the University of North Carolina, Chapel Hill, honors both tradition and deliberate reform. Further, it considers writing—and undergraduate teaching—central to its academic mission. It is thus fitting that writing is placed conventionally within the English department and taught by full-time faculty members. Because, as Birdsall explained, the faculty members cannot staff all the courses offered and because English has a vigorous graduate program, large numbers of graduate students also teach writing and share responsibility for the program. Occasionally, four or five part-time faculty members teach composition.

In 1979, in the spirit of considered but timely reform, the department advertised for a director of composition, looking for someone with credentials in the field. It found the best-qualified candidate close at hand. Erika Lindemann, having received her PhD in English from Chapel Hill in 1972, was directing the writing program at the University of South Carolina, Columbia. In that position, she had made a serious commitment to the study of composition. Her work in that field, together with her experience directing a writing program, prepared her for the appointment at her alma mater. She took the position, giving up tenure as an associate professor.

Lindemann, now once again a tenured associate professor, is described by a colleague as "one of the best appointments we've made in the last ten years." She teaches two courses a year and manages a program that offers three hundred sections of three freshman and three advanced courses, enrolling 6,500 to 7,000 students each year (on a campus of 22,000). She has gained respect for her work as a faculty member and as director of the program, and she has given the program firm direction. Her natural strategy and style in making changes have been especially appropriate for Chapel Hill. In her administration, as in her scholarship, Lindemann reaches for excellence, which she achieves carefully and deliberately.

Though Lindemann works gradually and carefully, she does indeed effect dramatic change. Doris Betts, chair of the faculty in 1984–85 and former director of the program, said to me, "I used to do the job that she has transformed." Betts described the changes Lindemann has made as director, winning support and understanding for the program and improving the conditions for teaching in it.

As Betts explained, Lindemann's work with teaching assistants has not only strengthened the program but also reduced graduate students' "normal paranoia." The process for hiring TAs has become "detailed and clear, [but not] mechanical." Once hired, TAs now receive considerably more help with their teaching than they formerly did. The staff manual and student guide are more detailed and helpful than before, with changes continually being introduced on the basis of experience. And Lindemann is doing more classroom visitation, more systematically. In addition, she and a colleague, Robert Bain, have begun teaching a graduate course in composition. (Betts has observed Lindemann's teaching, which she describes as superb.)

Lindemann has involved faculty members in making regular class visits, so that they remain acquainted with what goes on in freshman writing courses. Also, higher-level faculty members are now serving on the Freshman Committee. With this experience, "they can't sit back and say, 'They must not be teaching them to write over there.'"

Lindemann has earned the program a good place with the administration and faculty. She is honest, sensible, and pragmatic. She has been elected to the sixty-member Faculty Council (Chapel Hill's total faculty is two thousand) and has served on the council's Agenda Committee. Lindemann is active in what goes on across campus: she's interested in the Student Honor Court, for example, and the Reading Program. "At registration, she's there all day, doing the same kind of work as the TAs. That's the kind of leadership that works best." Lindemann is also active in public service, as was noted in an article appearing in the Raleigh paper shortly before my visit: she directs a summer writing program for teachers, and during the year she also works with the high school teachers given internships in the department.

Finally, Lindemann is much more active professionally than former directors, having published in the field and belonging to professional organizations. Composition is her scholarly specialty. Betts predicts that she will become a full professor—and she describes Lindemann as being "admired and liked by everybody."

Ramona Cook, Lindemann's administrative assistant, echoed Betts's comments on changes in the program. Cook explained how much the newly strengthened training program has drawn on existing resources and practices: these include an informal mentor system, faculty reviews of graded papers, workshops and orientation, and an idea file in the TA office. She also showed me parallels between the work of these two directors: Doris Betts had an open-door policy, and she initiated a "bottomless memo," a continuing memo to her staff. Lindemann has maintained the open-door policy, and in her own style she communicates often and easily with the faculty. Cook described Lindemann as extremely understanding and fair. "She has rules, and she sticks to her rules for everybody. . . . Everybody is treated the same, regardless of status."

These conversations with Betts and Cook confirmed what I saw in Lindemann's work: she knows how to use existing structures, finding their strengths and adding resilience. Chapel Hill's program as it now exists maintains the traditions and many of the practices of the past. At the same time, it reflects Lindemann's professional interests and personal abilities. The department and the university provide the context for an effective program, which Lindemann urges into being. As Betts told me, Lindemann is good at "wise delegating." She has brought others into decision making, granting "participatory leadership." And those working with her are "very loyal to her."

The primary vehicle for administering the program and ensuring its quality is the Freshman Committee. This is a nine-member committee made up of six graduate students and three faculty members teaching freshman courses and sharing responsibility for them. Each of the three freshman courses is overseen by a subcommittee of two graduate students and one faculty member, all of whom teach the course. The subcommittee designs the syllabus, selects the texts for the course, helps train and supervise TAs, and acts as a liaison between those teaching the course and the director. Faculty members are appointed by the chair, with Lindemann's advice, and graduate students are elected to the committee by their peers.

Weldon Thornton, professor of English and chair of the committee that conducted the curriculum review, told me that he taught the same texts and syllabus as new TAs when he taught English 1 and served on the Freshman Committee. Thus, a faculty member working closely with certain TAs is teaching the same course as they are. The subcommittee holds important responsibility for describing the course, then for supporting those who are teaching it. Toward these ends, the subcommittee helps prepare the course description and syllabus presented in the staff manual each year. The syllabus and manual, one of the committee members told me, thus offer "an overview of collected attitudes toward composition."

The strength of the committee lies in its responsibility for the program: this is a representative group, assigned to manage individual freshman courses and to serve as a liaison with its instructors. Its weakness, according to a current member, is its division into three working subcommittees, a division that sometimes "makes it hard to sense [that this is] one program." This comment suggests that to some extent the program as an entity still depends on the mind and presence of its director. The Freshman Committee, for example, manages the three freshman courses (English W, 1, and 2) but does not coordinate the three advanced writing courses (English 30, 32, and 33), which are administered by separate committees. (Creative-writing courses are administered separately within the English department.) In a program of this size, with faculty members and a hundred TAs teaching six courses, participatory governance works effectively, but not without careful leadership. The direction of this program is an exercise in freedom and control, the strength of the committee matching Lindemann's but never substituting for it.

This—or any—writing program derives its character from its staff as well as from its administrative structure and strategies. At Chapel Hill, all classes are taught by faculty members and teaching assistants in the English department. The problems associated with staffing, then, are not those of using temporary faculty members: instead, they are those of integrating regular faculty members into a writing program and of training and supervising an extremely large staff of TAs. To understand the role of faculty members and TAs in Chapel Hill's program, I spoke with administrators, the department chair, faculty members, and TAs, in addition to the director herself, and I reviewed materials produced within the program. As with any program review, this study not only showed me a cross section of the program as it fits within the university but also reminded me how many levels there are to any reality, how many perspectives on it.

At North Carolina, Chapel Hill, faculty members teach writing because of university traditions and departmental policy. Within the past few years, as we have seen, university committees have reaffirmed that the entire faculty shall be committed to teaching as well as research, to undergraduate as well as graduate education. These principles are evident in the teaching assignments made in the English department: the previous chair, James Gaskin, began the practice of assigning every faculty member at least one writing course a year. Ironically, the broad curricular reform to strengthen undergraduate education—in particular, the increase in the number of literature offerings—worked together with faculty retirements to reduce the frequency of writing-course assignments to one every two years. However, the present chair, Joseph Flora, not only maintains the policy of having faculty members teach writing but also sets an example by teaching a writing course every year.

Certainly the administration views this policy as a good one that should be made better known to the public. William Graves, the associate dean for general education, values always having some faculty members aware of what's going on in the writing program. Besides demonstrating departmental support for the program, he says, it "keeps Erika on her toes and gives her a sounding board." To Graves, the issue of whether or not the faculty members are better teachers than the graduate students is not as important as that of whether or not full-time faculty members are regularly involved in undergraduate teaching.

How do faculty members feel about teaching writing? Robert Bain pointed out that some faculty members—those near retirement, for example—are excused from the assignment. Beyond that, "There's a lot of grumbling. Some think it a waste of time. On the other hand, a good many people enjoy that work." Another faculty member I spoke with questioned whether assigned writing courses represent the best use of faculty resources. He thought that the policy might be "a public relations ploy as much as anything." He did think that the faculty should bear some responsibility for supervising the program, and he found the Freshman Committee—a departmental committee—one very good way to do that. It's all right, he felt, if some don't serve, so long as others are willing to do so. From what he had told me about his own work on the committee, it was clear that he himself had done an extremely conscientious job.

Several experienced TAs sounded almost cynical about faculty involvement in teaching writing. They pointed out that faculty members generally teach advanced courses and that some of those teaching freshman courses give the committee difficulty over the syllabus. Some, they felt, object to teaching writing at all. In their view, moreover, such faculty members do the job less well than do TAs interested in the assignment and in composition. While they thought the faculty-involvement policy had been good for the program, they were not sure how good it had been for students.

Other TAs volunteered support for the practice: one mentioned that it was important to him to find an assignment or some other material in the idea file that had been prepared by a professor of Old English—someone whose office was just down the hall. Some TAs would like to see faculty members who teach freshman composition come to their meetings, and they would like to see the faculty members on the Freshman Committee become as important a liaison as the student members are. They see the faculty members less often and seem to find them less available.

Finally, Doris Betts and Joseph Flora offered persuasive arguments for involving faculty members in the writing program. Betts observed that three former directors, all full professors, remain in the department; a fourth has become dean at another university. Having the faculty teach writing, she said, is "good as an idea" because it keeps the faculty informed and shows that the university and the department take writing seriously. Flora gave this historical perspective: when it was announced that all faculty members would teach composition once a year, older members said they knew nothing about such courses; now that all assistant professors begin by teaching composition during their first year, that situation can never recur. Those who want to teach during the summer often teach composition.

The practice of having faculty members teach writing is symbolically important—to the university, to the department, and to the program. Practically, it's both important and problematic. Even so, it shows that the program fits within the department. That connection is demonstrated and strengthened by Lindemann's presence in the department. She has earned credit as a colleague: now tenured, she may win promotion to full professor. Because her interests and work are seen as legitimate and professional, her example may in turn help to reinforce the faculty's interest in teaching writing.

Within the department, no one seems to ask whether or not teaching assistants should teach writing. Since the faculty can't cover all the sections scheduled and since large numbers of PhD candidates need training and experience in the classroom, naturally graduate students will teach freshman—and sometimes advanced—writing courses. The basic questions raised by the administration or the public are whether or not regular faculty members are involved in undergraduate teaching and whether or not graduate students are well qualified for this assignment. The answer to the first question is clearly yes, and the department and the program director work hard to ensure that the answer to the second is also yes. There are a hundred TAs on the staff, with twenty-five to thirty new appointments every year. Every TA holds a master's degree. As I spoke with people about the TAs' role in the writing program, the primary issues addressed were the nature and quality of their preparation and teaching and the fit between their teaching and their own graduate study. Again, the concerns and the attitudes expressed relate clearly to individual vantage points.

The TA program earns praise from the administration. Stephen Birdsall, concerned with educational quality, said that it is important to have coherent preparation for instructors and that it takes skill and commitment to oversee an effective training program. Lindemann, he feels, does a "marvelous job of overseeing and fine-tuning" the program in English. He commented on "almost constant review" and Lindemann's "alertness, flexibility, and effort to maintain oversight." Lindemann and her colleagues, he said, do not assume that they've found the right way to do things but feel that they should keep looking carefully at the program. Don Jicha, associate dean of the General College, observed that of all the departments using TAs in direct instruction, his office has encountered the fewest problems with English. He commended Lindemann's administration of the courses and the TAs' preparation and teaching. He also remarked that some TAs give better courses than faculty members would.

The faculty members I spoke with seem convinced of the quality of the training program and of the teaching done by TAs. Both Doris Betts and Robert Bain commented on the excellent teaching they saw when they visited TAs' classes in connection with applications for fellowships and lectureships. Bain said that he found some of them "better than regular faculty—and this is a good teaching faculty." Weldon Thornton said, "Erika's tough. She won't let some back in the classroom. The quality of instruction is good."

In the department's graduate program, there is one problem that the advanced TAs experience keenly: the difficulty of maintaining support. Although TAs may teach for four to seven years, depending on how many sections they teach each year, some TAs become ineligible the year before they complete their dissertations. There are two positions on this matter. Setting a maximum total number of thirteen to fifteen sections that graduate students can teach encourages them to complete the degree within a limited period of time. What is important is to handle the decisions fairly and to ensure the fairness and openness of the procedures. But some TAs affected by the limit, established in 1981, feel that there are too few lectureships and teaching fellowships available to those ineligible for teaching assistantships. In 1984, twenty applied for four lecturer positions, awarded to ABD students, and those not appointed could not get loans because they were no longer taking courses. While this issue is before the department as a whole, rather than before the writing program specifically, it deserves mention because it does affect those working in the program. As much as Lindemann has done to regularize the TAs' appointments and review, it seems likely that the procedures and criteria for making lecturers' appointments will also become clear and methodical. The limit on the number of appointments, however, may well continue to be a problem, though the department may include this issue in its current review of the graduate program.

The TAs themselves take various positions in assessing the writing program and their performance in it. In large part, their judgments seem related to the length of time they have been in the program, although there are disagreements and differing points of view even within a single year's class of graduate students.

At the Writing Center, I happened into conversation with four graduate students, experienced TAs then working in the Writing Center. The Writing Center has a staff of nine: eight graduate students (including the director) and one undergraduate. They put in ten hours of tutoring a week, working with students on referral or request. Students may come from the writing program, they may be referred through the Freshman Academic Monitoring System in the General College (a central advising system for freshmen and sophomores), or they may have been assigned "composition conditional" grades, which require that they improve their writing in order to receive passing grades and which may be given for courses in any department. The Writing Center also works cooperatively with the reading and library programs on campus. Though the center is small, and though it has no separate budget, it does offer important support to the writing program, and graduate students value appointments to work there. Those who tutor at the center are both selected (by the director) and self-selected (by their own interests and abilities in teaching writing).

The tutors I spoke with said that they are treated professionally, that they are convinced this is a good program, and that the morale is exceptionally good. I heard this collection of opinions: "In the English department, graduate students are tested all the time, and you're conscious of the student-teacher relationship." "Erika treats you like a colleague—Erika and Mona [Cook]. And TAs talk to you about their classes and trade assignments. There's a spirit of community, a sense of connection with the director and the office. You don't feel that you're wallowing." "The whole sense, spirit, is so different from that in the academic program. It helps you get through the academics. You're grown up when you teach." "You'd think you'd be burned out if you taught. I think I'd be burned out if I hadn't taught." "The morale here is so good, I could hardly believe it when I came.... In the comp program, people are not cynical." "If you're going into academics, this is what you're going to do."

In this conversation, I also discovered how many demands tutors and teaching assistants face at Chapel Hill. Graduate students in English generally take two courses each semester. First-year teaching assistants teach one course each semester, but advanced TAs can teach two. The program requires written examinations in three periods of British and American literature, an oral examination in the student's major and minor, a meeting to approve the student's prospectus for the dissertation, and an oral defense of the completed dissertation. Given these pressures, the dedication and respect the tutors expressed for the writing program are remarkable.

In a meeting with ten experienced TAs, I again heard praise, sometimes more guarded. The response here seemed to range between enthusiasm and satisfaction. When I asked what in this program they valued so much that they would want to take it with them to another program, they named the Freshman Staff Manual; the orientation booklet *Teaching Writing*; the idea file, a collection of classroom materials; and the grading scale. They also mentioned the use of written comments in teaching and an attitude toward students: students don't make mistakes intentionally, and teachers should focus on teaching and not simply marking what's wrong. They also referred to the support they get from the Writing Center, Reading Program, and Counseling Center. And, finally, they said that they valued being able to influence decisions—on texts, syllabi, and the program itself. "We evaluate everything here. And then we evaluate the evaluation forms."

By contrast, the first-year TAs had varying responses. When I met with them at the conclusion of their meeting to assess their first year's work, some said that they were treated less professionally in the writing program than in the academic program and that the morale was lower in the writing program. "The esprit de corps in the graduate program is good, but in the composition program, I'm always on edge." (Here I am using notes taken by J. Y. Dunbar.) They also weren't sure how to answer my question about how well they thought they were teaching. TAs with experience at other schools seemed to appreciate this program for what it gives them or, occasionally, to resent the training or the attitude they met at Chapel Hill. Some seemed to want more leeway and to feel that they were dealt with condescendingly. At the same time, several called for even more precise and complete information on English 2, the second-semester writing course. As I had been told to expect, some also said they would rather teach literature than writing.

These complaints are viewed as typical of first-year TAs. Experienced TAs seem either to believe strongly that the program is an excellent one and an important part of their own work or to become less vocal or, for my visit, less visible. The Freshman Committee did say that those who don't like "our" approach would rather teach English 2, the course that gives them more freedom. The committee also said that TAs who don't like Lindemann's or the program's approach don't feel that they are represented by the Freshman Committee.

After meeting with the first-year TAs, I thought, "This is just the kind of articulate and concerned group Erika wants to work with." She encourages questioning as a healthy part of the program. The Freshman Committee also functions in this way, worrying about a lack of sequence between the courses and about the unity of the program. A committee member said, "I respect Erika for having this committee. We may not always make her job easier for her." The committee demonstrates its strength and value by its willingness to question and challenge what's being done. The new TAs show, first, some lack of perspective (which the committee also granted: "We don't know what's being done at other places") and, second, some of the tension of first-year teaching on any campus, particularly when that year coincides with the first year of graduate work there. I heard, for example, contradictory calls for more freedom and for more restraint (a more detailed syllabus for English 2 and more prepared handouts). In any large program, there will be disagreements, and the challenge is to hear them, to let them be articulated, and then to let them become constructive, either because they can be turned into correctives, modifications not anticipated, or because they at least guarantee continuing review and discussion of the important issues.

In the context of this understanding of the TAs' attitudes and their position in the writing program, we can appreciate the training they are given. To support the TAs and prepare them for teaching their classes, Lindemann and the Freshman Committee offer a two-day orientation session before the fall term begins and a series of workshops during the year. As the 1984-85 agenda for orientation shows, Lindemann and committee members divide responsibility for the sessions, introducing TAs to the freshman program and offering practical advice. In addition, the department chair and two deans also meet with the new TAs. Their presence indicates their concern for the program and allows TAs, before they begin teaching, to understand the place of the program in the department and the university. During the year, workshops are conducted on specific topics: prewriting, library tours, the teaching performance, grading, commenting, particular essay assignments, and planning English 2.

In addition to these required sessions, an elective graduate course is now available. Robert Bain explained that when he proposed such a course in the early seventies, he couldn't get the support or interest needed for instituting it. Yet, with the change in the job market, he was approached in the middle to late seventies and asked to design a course that would give graduate students advanced training in composition theory and practice. Bain and Lindemann now teach English 131, Rhetorical Theory and Practice, once a year. In this course, students study both classical and modern theories of rhetoric and composition and survey current composition studies. One important assignment is to read William Riley Parker's essay, "Where Do English Departments Come From?" which lets students know where the department, as well as the program and the course, comes from and keeps them from appearing in job interviews, as James J. Murphy warns, with no awareness of this history ("Rhetorical History" 4). Experienced TAs recognize that the course will be valuable to them when they apply for jobs. Those who have taken the course qualify for serving on the Freshman Committee.

Two additional elements of the TA program serve the double purpose of supervision and training. These are "folder reviews" and classroom visits. While most programs ask faculty advisers to observe TAs in the classroom and to review some marked papers, the program at Chapel Hill has modified and refined this system in important ways.

During their first term of teaching, all new TAs submit a collection of marked essays from their classes: three papers for each of three students in each class. These are carefully reviewed by Freshman Committee members, who write lengthy comments on their findings. Lindemann reviews these notes, and then committee members meet individually with the TAs to discuss their work. The process is described by an experienced TA as "painful but helpful," an experience that opened her eyes. Some share this attitude, while others point out the possible problems: those writing comments are not equally skillful, though Lindemann's check helps avoid difficulties; TAs preparing the folder write for the evaluator and not for the student, but doing so is a normal and important part of training. At its best, the system gives the TAs the same kind of assessment that they give their students: the written remarks should include clear acknowledgment (and reinforcement) of strengths as well as clear and constructive observations on weaknesses. This procedure is itself a means of building community and encouraging discussion of teaching strategies and practices.

During the first term, new TAs also receive classroom visits from Lindemann. The idea is traditional enough but not its execution. Lindemann has developed a system for these visits based on a meticulous log of everything that happens in class. When she enters the room, she makes a seating chart and numbers students according to their order of arrival. Then, as the hour progresses, she makes meticulous notes on everything that occurs in class, recording how questions and remarks begin, noting their substance, and describing all physical activity as well. "The human videotape," as the TAs describe her, makes a detailed, objective record of the class. Then Lindemann makes marginal notes to herself, indicating what she considers to be units of classroom discourse, listing what the TA has done well, and reminding herself of the problems she saw. Soon after the class, she meets with the TA to go over the objective record and, on the basis of that record, to offer her interpretation and suggestions. Even here, she follows the practice she advises TAs to use in responding to student writing: she opens by saying, "You do this well," then she goes on to say, "I don't know whether you are conscious of this, but. . . ."

The TAs I spoke with were tremendously impressed with this system and grateful for it. One first-year TA had entered the graduate program after eighteen years of teaching in the high schools. She found the class log was the most valuable element of the yearlong training program. "Combined with the Freshman Committee's review of my paper comments, it has resulted in tremendous growth for me as a teacher this year." Through this training program, Lindemann stays very closely in touch with the work of her TAs, no small accomplishment given the numbers she is dealing with.

The effect Lindemann's program has on the graduate students teaching in it can be gauged by the remarks of a tutor at the Writing Center. When asked whether she would want to teach writing after receiving the PhD, she made this comment:

> I would want to continue teaching writing. Maybe half and half. . . . To teach literature is to teach writing. This represents a change in attitude: when I was studying, if students couldn't write, the professor would say he had to spoil a class to talk about writing. It looks like we'll all be teaching comp. We might as well teach it well. It's a good feeling when it goes well.

One further element of the program calls for our attention, both because it contributes to TA training and because it suggests how writing is taught in this program. That is the current Freshman Staff Manual, which sets forth the assumptions, principles, methods, and ends of the freshman courses. The manual itself is the descendant of many others used in the program. (I reviewed, for example, the manuals prepared for 1970-71 and 1979-80.) Yet, as with other features of the program, it has become a new thing in Lindemann's hands.

In the introduction to the manual, Lindemann places the writing courses in a context—historical, philosophical, pedagogical. She places Chapel Hill's writing courses in the rhetorical tradition, tracing briefly the changes in attitudes and approaches to teaching composition that have occurred during this century. She also states clearly her own assumptions about writing and her expectations for the program. Here, Lindemann addresses the teaching assistants as students and teachers—and as writers. She outlines their duties and explains the resources available to them. After a long section on plagiarism, added recently by committee members, the manual offers nineteen pages under the title "Teaching—An Introduction." Here, teachers find advice on preparing for the first day of class, planning class time, and assigning and marking papers. Robert Bain's "A Framework for Judging" (307-09) appears within this section of the text.

Reasonableness and a commitment to considered change characterize the language in the Freshman Staff Manual. Revised annually, the manual reflects the "cumulative, shared wisdom" of past and present teachers, Freshman Committee members, and program directors. Throughout the manual the writing is open, direct, informed, controlled, and substantive. It easily combines imperatives and advice, encouragement and warning, theory and practical wisdom. The manual attempts to help TAs understand the reasons for teaching writing and for teaching it with care. Note, simply, this paragraph from the 1984-85 manual:

> Prior to the 1950's, the teaching of writing had been synonymous with the teaching of grammar, a prescriptive grammar codified during the eighteenth-century's mathematically inclined "Age of Reason." Although poets like Chaucer, for example, had liberally sprinkled sentences with "not" and "ne" to intensify the negation, eighteenth-century grammarians, borrowing a principle from mathematics, legislated against double negatives. Observing furthermore that Latin infinitives are one word, they also proscribed the split infinitive on the assumption that what was "logical" for Latin must also be logical for English. Doubtless the writing courses you and your teachers took contained heavy doses of traditional, prescriptive grammar. (2)

Here, Lindemann presents something of the history of teaching writing, and she attempts to explain to teaching assistants some of the perspective they may bring to the task. She wants them to understand their own assumptions and the broad historical context of their work.

But she also wants them to understand the implications of the decisions they may make in teaching their classes, marking their students' papers, and assigning final grades. She shares practical wisdom in advising them on when to fail students. Essentially, she says, don't pass English 1 students if you'll be embarrassed to be identified as their teacher when they do poorly in English 2. But remember, when you're teaching English 2, that there may have been extenuating circumstances in English 1.

Members of the Freshman Committee take responsibility for the material in each of the courses. Surprisingly, the nature and structure of the courses are quite firmly fixed. Set syllabi are provided, and the courses are of clearly prescribed types. English W is a basic writing course, English 1 is based on the traditional modes of discourse, and English 2 is focused on argumentative prose. From discussions on campus, however, I learned that faculty members and experienced TAs can propose alternative texts or syllabi and that the courses themselves are subject to reasoned and gradual change. In this way, Lindemann maintains a certain control over the program and ensures consistency from classroom to classroom, at the same time welcoming new information and new ideas.

Though syllabi are prescribed, alternatives are offered in texts, types of papers, and the use of the syllabi. The manual thus reveals a director who is experienced in teaching and writing about composition and who is comfortable sharing responsibility with a committee. In its structure and its overall accomplishment, the manual shows clearly both the director's authority and the influence of the Freshman Committee.

The manual sends teaching assistants a message something like this: The teaching of writing is a sophisticated practice, grounded in theory, history, and research. You can do it, and you can do it well. Those of us preparing the manual know more about teaching writing than you do right now, and we've reached consensus on how it should be done, but we trust you to carry it out and gradually to develop your own variations, your own distinctive style and practice. This work is important: it matters to your students now and throughout their careers, and it matters to you, personally and professionally. You should do it well and with dignity, and it will be a good experience for you. You begin as a novice who needs instruction and support, but you join a community; it is a sharing community, and you will make your own contributions to your students and to your peers. You will be called to account, but you will be judged fairly. You will know what's expected, and you will be given direction and help. You will be treated with the same respect we want you to give your students.

Thus, teaching assistants are given the reasons for the type of program and the approach to teaching writing that the manual describes. They are also given full information on the courses as they are expected to teach them. Let us take English W as an example.

English W, Basic Writing, is designed for students who have "persistent problems with organization, paragraph or sentence structure, and the conventions of edited English" (1984-85 Freshman Staff Manual 42). The manual presents and explains these assumptions:

1. We learn writing best by doing it.
2. Because all writers review and change their drafts, students should rewrite assignments before submitting them to the teacher.
3. Although students should write frequently and receive frequent responses to their work, not all of their writing needs a grade.
4. The required essay assignments in English W remain roughly parallel to assignments in English 1, each student writing five papers rather than the usual eight.
5. Although students need practice controlling the conventions of edited English, the grammar instruction they receive in English W should be functional; that is, it should be practical, not theoretical, enabling a student to "do" English and not just to know "about" English.
6. Since the abilities to read and write reinforce each other, W students strongly recommended for the Reading Program must participate in it. (43–44)

The aims of English W are described in this way:

1. to give students guided practice in planning, drafting, and rewriting narrative and expository essays of 300-450 words,
2. to help students gain confidence and fluency in their use of edited English,
3. to encourage students to use the Reading Program,
4. to help students improve their vocabularies. (44)

Following a discussion of these aims, together with the texts and methods for achieving them, the manual offers a week-by-week syllabus, descriptions of the five papers to be assigned, and a discussion of the duties of English W staff members—evaluating exemption essays and attending staff meetings.

Lindemann explained that this basic course has gradually been changed from a grammar course to a writing course. To accomplish this change, Lindemann worked closely with the staff until they became willing to teach the course in a new way and were well prepared to do so. That course, now in their hands, is still changing. She told me that she believes in working with people, to change attitudes and thinking and to allow them to make changes, rather than in creating "we-they" situations.

This course description is followed by other course descriptions written by other members of the committee. The emphasis on process that now characterizes English W has also entered English 1 and English 2. The modes course, then, is already something other than traditional. Here is the discussion of modes in the staff manual:

The papers are defined as traditional modes of discourse (definition, classification, etc.). Although these are useful modes for the college writer, these norms should not be treated as formulaic structures, as ends in themselves, but as ways of organizing the students' own thoughts, opinions and ideas into coherent written expression. The expository modes are building blocks to use in assembling these personal statements; the modes themselves are *heuristics* that enable the writer to discover what questions most effectively develop concrete details for writing on particular types of topics. Making a means of discovery the basis of the various writing assignments in English 1 should develop in the students a skill which they will carry with them throughout their college years and beyond. (57)

At the end-of-the-year meeting with first-year TAs, Lindemann fielded their questions about the use of the modes, the number of papers assigned, and the timing of the research-paper assignment. The questions raised, she told me, would never have come up a few years ago. Now she takes them as a mandate for review of the courses, just the kind of review she would welcome and will encourage the Freshman Committee to initiate.

In the year following this study Erika Lindemann planned to be on leave to do her own research and writing in composition. In her absence Robert Bain would direct the program—a program so strong and self-sufficient that he would serve, he said, merely "as a shopkeeper." Lindemann, though, looks for continuing change, generated by Bain, the Freshman Committee, or the faculty and TAs. Within the next few years, certainly, she expects to see definite change in the descriptions and curricula of the freshman courses and perhaps in the training program, too. Unless the university receives external funding (already once denied), Lindemann does not expect to begin special efforts at writing across the curriculum: she will continue to answer specific requests, and the Writing Center will go on serving some students from across campus as well as helping faculty members develop writing projects for students in other disciplines.

One important change Lindemann would like to see would be within the program's administrative staff. She needs an assistant director, and though the department once advertised the position without making an appointment, Lindemann and many of those working with her recognize the need for this addition to the staff. Whether the department will accept a composition specialist or will prefer a literary scholar with interest in composition may show whether the department at this time is inclined more toward tradition or reform.

Agenda for Campus Visit

Monday, 15 April 1985

5:00   Erika Lindemann, director of composition

Tuesday, 16 April 1985

   8:00   Freshman Committee

   9:00   Robert Bain, 1985-86 director of composition

 10:00   Trish Ward, director of the Writing Center

 11:30   Weldon Thornton, committee chair for campus self-study

 12:30   Jo Tarvers, Emily Seelbinder, and Susan Landstrom, teaching assistants

   2:00   Joseph Flora, chair of the English department

   2:30   Teaching assistants, teaching fellows, lecturers

   5:00   Erika Lindemann and Ramona Cook, administrative assistant

Wednesday, 17 April 1985

   9:00   William Graves, associate dean for general education

 10:00   Stephen Birdsall, acting dean of arts and sciences

 10:30   Don Jicha, associate dean of the General College

 11:00   Doris Betts, chair of the Faculty Council

 12:30   Erika Lindemann

   3:00   First-year teaching assistants and Mellon-Babcock interns

   5:00   Erika Lindemann and Robert Bain

Materials Reviewed

University Committees

Graves, William, Chair, et al. Annual Report of the Educational Policy Committee, including a Special Report on the Quality of Undergraduate Education, to Be Considered at a Special Meeting of the Faculty Council, 22 Apr. 1983.

Leutze, James R., and Weldon Thornton. Draft of the Report of the Teaching Assistants Subcommittee, undated.

Ornstein, P. A. Memo to members of Task Group X, 4 Sept. 1984.

Task Group X of the 1984 University Self-Study, Final Report: The Quality of Undergraduate Education Appropriate to a Research University, Dec. 1984.

Program Manuals

The Freshman Staff Manual, 1979-80.

Freshman Staff Manual, 1984-85.

Information for Instructors of Freshman English, 1970-71.

The Student Guide to Freshman English, 1983-84.

Program and Department Materials

Conditions of Appointment: information and agreements for teaching assistants.

English Course Evaluation: sample forms.

English Internship Program, 1984-85: announcement.
English 131, Spring 1985: syllabus, Robert Bain.
English 300, Contemporary Rhetoric: syllabus, Erika Lindemann.
English Writing Sample: information and scoring guides.
Enrollment figures for writing courses offered between 1978 and 1985.
Freshman Staff Orientation, 20-21 Aug. 1984: agenda.
Graduate Studies Program, Department of English, the University of North Carolina at Chapel Hill.
Guide to Graduate Studies, Department of English, July 1984.
Guidelines and agreement for tutors.
Guidelines for English 131 projects.
Guidelines for review of TAs' folders of sample papers.
"The Improvement of Teacher Education at Chapel Hill," *News from the Graduate School*, Spring 1985.
Materials for UNC Writing Workshop.
1984-85 Workshops and Staff Meetings: schedule.
Teaching Assistants, 1984-85: roster.
Teaching Writing, prepared for freshman staff orientation, 20-21 Aug. 1984.
Writing and Foreign Language Workshops, Summer 1985: announcement.

Director's Memos and Reports

Memo to all first-year TAs, 24 Sept. 1984: folders of student papers for review.
Memo to all TAs, 4 Apr. 1985: book fair.
Memo to English graduate students, 1 Feb. 1985: teaching assistantships.
Memo to Joseph M. Flora, 6 Nov. 1984: comparison of 1980 freshmen with 1984 freshmen.
Memo to the staff, 10 Apr. 1985: elections to the Freshman Committee.
Memo to the staff, 22 Apr. 1985: grades.
Memos to all teaching assistants, 4 and 10 Apr. 1985: sign-up for Fall 1985 courses.
Report on graduate teaching assistants in English, 1983-84.
Sample class logs and comments, together with letter to the author, 21 Apr. 1985.
Sample memo: teaching observation.

Other Letters and Memos

Betts, Doris. Bottomless Memo to Staff, 28 Aug. 1976–.
———. Bottomless Memo to Staff, 24 Nov. 1976.
———. The Bottom Memo, 13 Dec. 1977.
Cook, Mona. Memo to the staff, 18 Apr. 1985: end-of-term notices.
Williamson, Samuel R., Jr. Letter to Erika Lindemann, 6 June 1984: terms of appointment.

Notes on TA Meetings

Dunbar, J. Y. Unedited field notes on experienced TAs' meeting with the author, 16 Apr. 1985, and on first-year TAs' meeting, 17 Apr. 1985.
Rickard, John. Notes on first-year TAs' end-of-year meeting, 17 Apr. 1985.

CHAPTER 9

The University of Pennsylvania

A T THE UNIVERSITY of Pennsylvania, two writing programs are based in the English department: David Espey directs a large freshman seminar program, enrolling more than two thousand students each year, and Peshe Kuriloff directs a new cross-curricular program, as well as a writing center. The two writing programs, at different stages of evolution, are designed on similar principles. The freshman seminars are conducted by teaching assistants who, after apprenticeship and training, design the syllabi for their courses; as a result, the materials and themes of the courses often reflect the TAs' research interests. Writing across the University (WATU) is staffed by graduate students from various disciplines who work as consultants or teaching assistants in courses often directly related to their own fields of study. Participation in these programs is voluntary: freshmen may elect English seminars to apply toward satisfaction of the humanities requirement, and faculty members may affiliate their courses with WATU. Thus, both programs encourage graduate students to make connections between their study and their teaching, and both invite rather than require participation.

While the freshman program has for some time been important to an undergraduate education at Penn, the interdisciplinary program has quickly gained attention and prestige. In its third year at the time of this study, it has strong endorsement from both the administration and the faculty. This program has won unusual favor not only because it parallels the existing freshman program but also because it fits this university exceptionally well. A study of Penn's writing programs, then, should begin with attention to their university context and their history.

During her initial phone interview, Peshe Kuriloff said, "The entire Penn community, with support from the administration, is working to make excellent writing a priority in all departments." She also explained that this effort fits directly within the provost's goals for Penn in the 1980s. When I met with the provost, Thomas Ehrlich, he confirmed that Writing across the University is especially appropriate at Penn: this new interdisciplinary program is considered important to the mission of the university.

A planning document prepared for the faculty of Arts and Sciences in March 1983 states three goals, including the enhancement of educational programs. The statement on increasing the academic excellence and intellectual vigor of undergraduate programs begins in this way: "It is crucial that we continue to offer our undergraduate students an education that will fulfill their professional goals. In so doing we are committed to improving the writing skills of our students, to developing courses which require the use of the computer, and continuing to develop interdisciplinary courses and programs . . . " (enclosed with memo from Donald D. Fitts, acting dean, to Peter Conn, associate dean for undergraduate studies, et al., 7 Mar. 1983). This statement reflects the priorities stated in "Choosing Penn's Future," a strategic plan that Sheldon Hackney, the university's president, presented to the trustees in January 1983 ("President's Report 1983," *Almanac* 15 Nov. 1983: 2).

As Joel Conarroe, outgoing dean of the School of Arts and Sciences, said to me, Writing across the University (WATU) matches "with stunning appropriateness . . . what the president and provost have in mind for the university as a whole." He explained, "The signature of Penn is the opportunity for cutting across disciplinary boundaries. We have twelve schools, one place. The four undergraduate schools share students, classes, and a common intellectual experience. We have the opportunity for one university, and the administration wants to make this known." He added, "Students are attracted by the diversity of intellectual opportunity. This program is a symbol of it." Conarroe considers this a very good program, its impact incalculable.

Thomas Ehrlich explained the program's origin in this way:

> Students had been getting a lot of writing experience in the freshman seminars, but they had a hard time translating that experience . . . into writing for sociology, psychology, political science. They needed help with discipline-specific writing. Faculty members in other departments were concerned, but they said they had no expertise in teaching writing. The Writing Center offers remediation and help with writing generally, but it takes initiative to get there. . . . English said we want to help—and in this they were different from English departments at [other universities], departments that would say, "If you want our help, you come here." This plan would help our graduate students too, financially and [intellectually, giving them] experience in working with students' writing in various disciplines.

The person most responsible for the English department's position is Robert Lucid, who chaired the department from 1980 to 1985. Lucid explained that the emphasis on writing began with a departmental self-study, an effort to produce a priority report, five years ago. With an outgoing president, an acting provost, and an acting dean, Lucid thought that the department should decide what part it was going to play in the historical process of administrative change. He urged the department "to decide what we were about as an entity and as an entity within the School of Arts and Sciences," for he saw this as "a good time to look at what we should become as a department."

The departmental priority committee tried to judge the department's potential with respect to writing as a practical curricular question. As Lucid said, "None of us knew a lot about it. We brought in Elaine Maimon as a consultant, and we quickly saw [we had] a lot of expanding to do here." People outside the department were uncertain what should be done. The Student Committee on Undergraduate Education was calling for a return to the composition requirement, and some outside faculty members also felt that the department should simply "beef up freshman English." But Lucid knew that Penn already had a strong freshman English program: students' skills were declining over a four-year period of undergraduate work. Lucid thought that the effort to improve writing needed a much broader base than could be provided by English alone. It became clear that this program would require new funds and new support.

Elaine Maimon credits Lucid with providing the initiative for creating a new program. The attempt to improve writing, she said, "had to do with Bob's vision, [with] what he wanted to do as chair." He wanted the department's action "to have university-wide implications." She pointed out that Lucid has a good deal of influence at the university. He had been president of the Faculty Senate for two terms, and he could influence other department chairs. Conarroe, too, said that the success of the program "is a measure of Lucid's leadership: he thought it important and made it so for the department."

Acting on Maimon's suggestions, Lucid immersed himself in the literature on writing across the curriculum. Clearly, Maimon's expertise influenced the programs at Penn. She brought to the discussions not only her knowledge of writing research, theory, and practices but also the example of innovative programs, like Yale's and her own at Beaver College. Maimon, who had earned her PhD at Penn, began serving as a consultant during 1981-82 to make initial plans for a cross-curricular program. During that year, the new provost began holding hearings to learn what departments were "on the edge of doing" (Lucid). Because of the administration's interest in broad undergraduate areas, the English department's presentation on writing "knocked them flat," Lucid reported. As a result, the department was able to make structural changes.

In the past, an assistant professor had been given released time to direct the freshman seminars and manage the small Writing Center. With new support, the department created a position for a full-time administrator to direct the writing program. Tim Martin, who had recently earned his PhD in English at Penn, was appointed to that post. He coordinated the freshman program and also helped design WATU, which he then directed. In addition, Peter Conn, a member of the department and at the time associate dean of undergraduate studies, developed a new course for graduate students in their first term of teaching. Conn and Humphrey Tonkin, also a department member, participated in Maimon's summer program at Beaver College. Maimon herself continued acting as a consultant through the spring of 1983, holding a half-time appointment at Penn during 1982-83.

When Martin left to accept a faculty appointment at another university, Lucid divided the position, making two full-time appointments: Kuriloff to direct WATU and the expanding Writing Center, Espey to direct the freshman seminars and act as administrative liaison with the graduate chair of the department. Through Espey's appointment, Lucid could reinforce the link between graduate students' study and their teaching.

Lucid reported that the faculty, both within and outside the School of Arts and Sciences, feel that WATU is a solid program, one that is long overdue. He pointed out that the freshman seminars and WATU are the only horizontal programs at Penn, and very good ones. The provost also spoke of WATU as a program that infuses the curriculum. Given the resurgence of interest in the undergraduate curriculum, he argued, each institution has to build on its own comparative advantages. The strength of Penn is its links between liberal arts and the professions, and WATU is a mechanism for reaching throughout the curriculum.

At Penn, it seems extremely important that the impetus and support for this particular program have come from English and have come in response to a new administration's interest in strategic planning. Because the program embodies the "one university" concept the administration emphasizes, it has quickly taken on symbolic importance. With a new president and a new provost stressing the connections between parts of the university and looking for far-reaching and innovative programs, WATU has been attractive, even compelling, as an effort to improve undergraduate education and to cross departmental lines in doing so. At the same time, English has provided the departmental base the program needs for both administrative and intellectual purposes. Thomas Ehrlich emphasized the importance of the program's being housed in English. He said that although Penn is more interdisciplinary than many other universities, it is still rooted in departments. David Espey, too, said, "If you don't have a department at Penn, you don't have a home."

Within the English department, the response to the program has been quite positive, though most of the faculty are involved only casually. In fact, the department has endorsed a tenure or tenure-track appointment in composition. Unfortunately, in the same year as that endorsement, the administration said the department "must do more with less" (Lucid). The department was given only one position, though it had a number of openings, including one in Renaissance. As a result, no faculty appointment has been made in composition. Yet, even without faculty appointments in composition, Lucid feels that the writing program should be inside English, where it is protected. The program also has a good effect on the department, Lucid said, for "it keeps the department from parochial high-culturalism: from simply rising above things that, though elementary, are real and important." Clearly, Lucid's initiative and his effectiveness as an academic leader have profoundly influenced the stature of the program.

For a program that is still quite young, WATU has gained unusual recognition and support from the faculty and administration. But while it suits the ideology and the structure of its institution, it does not yet have a solid financial base. There are two reasons, which are related:

1. The program has received external funding during its first three years. Twice Penn submitted a major grant proposal for funding to cover all expenses for the program as it now exists and for an even broader, more ambitious program of Humanities across the University. When this grant was denied, Penn had to make other arrangements. With support and advice from the provost and dean, the development office has found generous support from individuals and corporations. These include the CIGNA Foundation, Chemical Bank, Martin Lipton, Richard Fisher, and now the AT&T Foundation. After three years, however, WATU is no longer a "brave new program" (Conarroe) that can be funded year by year, and there is increasing pressure to find the assured funding needed for planning and continuity.

2. During the program's early years, the new administration carefully reviewed the finances of the university. In his "President's Report 1983," Sheldon Hackney included this statement as one of four planning maxims: "The University must conserve its resources and protect its financial integrity" (*Almanac* 15 Nov. 1983: 2). Accordingly, each of the twelve schools must strive to become financially sound in its own right. (As one faculty member put it, "Each tub on its own bottom.") While some schools—the School of Education, for example—now make a profit, the School of Arts and Sciences has a substantial deficit and for that reason did not yet have an approved budget for 1985-86 when I was on campus in late April 1985. Obviously, it will not be easy to add the writing program to the university's regular budget, particularly that for Arts and Sciences.

There seem two possible solutions to the problem. First, the program has submitted, as an interim measure, a new five-year grant proposal for foundation support and received a three-year commitment. This grant will partially fund the program and provide a base for planning and for continuing to expand the program. In fact, if the grant had not been made, much of the summer of 1985 would have gone into searching for other sources of support. Second, at some point the university may need—and be able—to assume the costs of the program. The provost recognizes the importance of finding regular funding. He told me that a writing program needs solid support of two kinds: (1) "It needs a group committed to making it work. Most writing centers are not within the mainstream of the university. If the departmental chair is committed to it, he stands up and says so. I don't think inherently there is any reason why it can't work outside the department; it's just harder." (2) "It needs a solid budgetary base. It needs to be built in on a permanent basis. That will happen here, though it's not done yet. It's easier to cut something that stands off to the side."

If the program were to be funded by the university, the question is how that funding should be provided. Joel Conarroe, looking at his budget, said it could not be funded by Arts and Sciences. It might even be argued that this program should regularly be provided for out of university funds. Robert Lucid, however, suggested an alternative plan that sounds persuasive. He recommends that the program receive funding from three sources: (1) Arts and Sciences, (2) schools and departments outside Arts and Sciences, and (3) external agencies. Ideally, Lucid said, the funding would be divided into equal thirds. He pointed to the current grant proposal as a means toward such an arrangement and cited the Wharton School of Business as one school that might begin contributing funds for collaborative projects. Lucid would, in fact, like to receive graduate support from the dean and also have a budget line in each participating department. These arrangements would offer organizational endorsement and thus help to institutionalize the program. His plan overall would allow for a division of responsibility and support.

While WATU has not yet found continuing financial support, it has clearly and quickly gained the departmental base and administrative support it needs. The program, then, has come to life in a welcoming environment, with good chances of success. Its financial pressures can limit that success, of course, both because they can threaten the program's life and because they force the director to spend much time concentrating on budgets and grant proposals. But it is in the context of university traditions and commitments that we can understand the academic vitality both of this program and of the freshman program that it complements.

Writing across the University

The stated goal of Penn's Writing across the University Program is "to promote excellence in writing in every academic discipline" (Program Description, Fall 1985). A grant proposal opens with these remarks:

> Writing is a powerful tool for learning in any discipline. It forces the student to become deeply engaged in a subject, to clarify connections between ideas, to refine thought and expression, and to pass along new knowledge to others. In its Writing Across the University Program, the University of Pennsylvania assumes that the ability to write clearly is essential to learning in every discipline. It sees writing as a skill which cannot be learned in isolation from subject matter, as if form and content were divisible. Consequently, Pennsylvania supports the position that writing should be assigned and evaluated in all parts of the curriculum and at every level of study—as an integral part of the intellectual enterprise in every discipline. (Proposal to the AT&T Foundation 1)

The program, then, is not a response to a perceived literacy crisis but an important element of an education at Penn. It is not viewed as remedial, and none of its courses or services are required. As the proposal states, the program works within Penn's "general climate of voluntarism": "the program makes attractive educational opportunities available to faculty, graduate student teaching assistants, and undergraduates by appealing to their own commitment to the achievement of excellence" (5-6).

WATU invites faculty members across campus to affiliate their courses with the writing program. In their courses, these faculty members emphasize writing as integral to learning the discipline. They also collaborate with a teaching assistant or writing consultant (both designated as writing fellows) to design course assignments toward this end. If a teaching assistant is normally assigned to the course, that TA becomes associated with WATU for training and advice and earns an additional $500 for the course. In other courses, a writing consultant is appointed by WATU to advise the instructor on writing assignments and perhaps also to visit the class, read papers, or hold conferences. For this work, the consultant receives $800. The consultant is an experienced teaching assistant who has already worked in an affiliated class. Thus, the writing fellows are graduate students from a variety of disciplines, including, but certainly not limited to, English.

The program's association with English, therefore, is primarily administrative. Peshe Kuriloff began directing the program in the fall of 1984, as Coordinator of Writing across the University and Coordinator of the Writing Center. Her appointment is in the English department, and she reports to the chair. Kuriloff was familiar with the program before assuming this position: she had taught advanced expository writing as a lecturer in English since 1979, when she received her PhD from Bryn Mawr, and she had acted as a consultant to WATU in 1983-84, helping Tim Martin train the writing fellows. Kuriloff had also taught academic and professional writing to school administrators enrolled in a special doctoral program in the Graduate School of Education, and she had served as a consultant to the Annenberg School of Communications. Thus, she brought to the position contacts and experience both within and beyond the English department.

In her first year as coordinator of the program Kuriloff continued the practices and maintained the structure of the program developed by Tim Martin. She has expanded the range of the program to include increasing numbers of schools and departments. In the spring of 1985, for example, forty-two courses were affiliated with WATU and were offered in these departments and schools:

American Civilization	Electrical Engineering
Anthropology	Folklore
Art History	Graduate School of Fine Arts
Biology	Health Care
Civil Engineering	History
Classical Studies	History and Sociology of
Communications	Science
Comparative Literature	International Relations
Economics	Management

Nursing	Psychology
Oriental Studies	Regional Science
Philosophy	Religious Studies
Political Science	Urban Studies

All four undergraduate schools—Arts and Sciences, Engineering, Wharton, and Nursing—were represented, and approximately fourteen hundred students were enrolled.

To prepare the writing fellows, Kuriloff conducted an orientation and training program based on Tim Martin's model. As she explained to the fellows, this training was designed to give them "a few basic skills, some background information and an appropriate attitude toward the task at hand," as well as to bring them together to discuss issues important to them. She told them directly that the assumption that anyone who writes well can teach others to write "has never made any sense." Instead, "the ability to teach students to write, like the ability to teach them anything, is a learned skill, and the goal of our training is to help you acquire that skill as effectively as possible" (Responsibilities of a Writing Fellow: Training 1).

In this training program, a one-day orientation session before each term begins is followed by a series of two-hour workshops. Fellows must attend at least three of the eight workshops offered each term, and they must participate in at least one. The workshop topics include assignments, responses to student writing, conferences, informal writing, writing and computing, collaborative learning, and composition theory. They are led not only by Kuriloff but also, it is important to note, by Linda Brodkey and Susan Lytle from the Graduate School of Education. Brodkey and Lytle represent teacher training and the doctoral program in writing offered in education. Brodkey, in fact, was hired in 1981 to design a series of courses in writing— teaching and research—for college and high school teachers. This connection with the work being done by the anthropologists, linguists, and sociolinguists in the School of Education strengthens and enriches the training program.

Another important element of that program is a colloquium series on writing conducted by teachers, scholars, and consultants from Penn and other universities and colleges. During 1984-85, for example, a panel discussion on teaching writing in the disciplines was presented by these Penn faculty members: Jacob Abel, professor of mechanical engineering and chair of the Faculty Senate; Ivar Berg, professor of sociology and associate dean for undergraduate studies; and Stephen Roth, professor and chair of biology. Other speakers have included Elaine Maimon, Kenneth Bruffee, Louise Rosenblatt, Drew Faust, Robert Lucid, Richard Marius, Norman Mailer, E. D. Hirsch, and Walter Ong. All writing fellows attend the colloquiums, conducted twice a year.

Fellows may also take courses cross-listed in the School of Education and the department of English. Reading and Writing Academic Prose, a course designed to teach advanced doctoral students how to turn assigned papers into publishable essays, has been offered twice. As a visiting professor, James Kinneavy offered a graduate-level course in rhetoric during the summer of 1984 and a second course the following summer.

In addition, a new and effective component of the training program was added in 1984-85. Kuriloff appointed senior fellows to work as counselors and guides for their colleagues. The senior fellows meet at least once a month with their fellows, grouped by disciplines, to offer advice and support and to act as liaisons between the fellows and others in the program. Because the senior fellows have offices in their own departments, they can easily meet with colleagues teaching in their own or related fields. John Benoit, a graduate student in American civilization and one of the first senior fellows, explained that he has learned more through consulting with his peers than through the formal training program, both because he's spent more time in this work and because he's helped his colleagues deal with problems they confront. His presence seems also to have been valuable to those working with him.

Given this training and support, writing fellows integrate writing into courses in various disciplines. TAs are expected to devote fifty hours a semester to their work and writing consultants, eighty hours. They spend twelve hours on training and three to six hours with the senior fellows, leaving three hours each week for TAs and five for consultants to give to their courses and students. Although the assignments and means of collaboration developed by the writing fellows and their faculty associates vary widely from course to course, Kuriloff listed these standard practices: constructing writing assignments, often together with the professor; discussing writing and Writing across the University in class; participating in class discussions; assigning informal writing projects for class or small-group meetings; discussing writing assignments with students; and reviewing and responding to drafts (Responsibilities of a Writing Fellow 1). Much broader involvement is also possible: Carol Schilling, a senior fellow who is a graduate student in English, has helped design and has team-taught Writing for Biologists, a course focused on grant proposals to the National Institute of Health. She taught the course with two biology professors, one the undergraduate chair of the department.

WATU extends its reach through the Writing Center and the Writing Lab. Both small units are administered by Kuriloff and related to her cross-curricular program. The Writing Center is staffed by graduate students, paid at an hourly rate. Beginning in 1984-85, the staff has been broadened to include students from disciplines other than English. During the fall semester, it was staffed by five graduate students in English, two in English as a second language, and five others in folklore, communications, comparative literature, American civilization, and history and sociology of science. They have all participated in the training program for writing fellows. At the time of this study plans for 1985-86 included inviting undergraduates to become peer tutors: outstanding students from the freshman seminars would be offered a special seminar on writing and collaborative learning to prepare for these appointments.

The Writing Center offers individual conferences to undergraduates, graduate students, and faculty members. During 1984-85, the staff saw 428 students, many of whom were enrolled in freshman English seminars. In the spring, because the enrollment in these seminars dropped from 1,550 to 460, the staff was reduced from twelve to nine and spent most of its time with students from other classes or levels. These included students from writing or affiliated courses; foreign graduate students; and students enrolled in humanities, social science, or business classes. Faculty members and graduate students writing their dissertations have also used the services of the Writing Center. Two members of the Writing Center staff are living in college houses and meeting with students in the residences.

The Writing Lab is a computer room adjacent to Kuriloff's office. The lab houses ten Radio Shack TRS-80 computers, given to the program by the math department. These are to be used exclusively for composing and revising on the word processor, and work-study students offer small-group workshops on these procedures. The lab is open to any member of the Penn community, but students enrolled in affiliated courses have priority.

While the resources for supporting writing across the curriculum are small and while writing fellows working in WATU have few hours to spend with their students, this effort to improve writing across campus seems to be taking effect. One of the senior fellows, Julie Dobrow, a graduate student in the Annenberg School of Communications, sees the program working on three levels. First, she said, WATU operates to make itself obsolete: after courses are affiliated with the program for a few years, they simply build in writing as a requirement. Second, graduate students working in the program learn its rhetoric and techniques, which they continue to use as students and teachers. Third, students begin writing more papers and learn to submit drafts for review and to revise their work.

The reports all fellows submit each term suggest that the program is having these effects on the work of undergraduate and graduate students. Students enrolled in affiliated courses are receiving individual attention to their writing, and they are being asked to write frequently and in a variety of ways. Graduate students are finding new approaches to teaching writing— and even to writing—that influence their own work. Fellows stress what they have learned about informal writing and about the writing process. They assign and review rough drafts, and they recognize the value of drafting in their own work. They ask students to make regular journal entries or to freewrite. They often remark on the value of conferences and say they have learned a good deal about commenting on student writing. John Benoit told me that graduate students in the program are becoming self-conscious about writing and also coming to see themselves as teachers. Some had never discussed their teaching with anyone until they became associated with this program. Through WATU, Benoit says, "Penn is establishing a tradition of TAs thinking about writing."

Letters of support received during the spring of 1985 also show that WATU is valuable to the faculty members whose courses are affiliated with it. Some stress the importance of the writing that is being done in their courses; others emphasize the assistance that the writing fellows give them. Together, they confirm that the program improves the quality of education at Penn in many ways. Here are some excerpts from these letters of endorsement:

Joy Pauschke, an assistant professor of civil engineering, values the help writing fellows give her students in a senior design course. "The [Civil Engineering] 470 report is the largest document the seniors write during their 4 years at Penn and is often presented to prospective employers during interviews. Hence, it is very important that not only the technical work be competent but also the writing and presentation be of 'Penn quality.'"

James Ross, a professor of philosophy, writes, "There is a special need, in disciplines such as philosophy, for students to get careful guidance in reading and writing. Ideally, such guidance involves a lot of short writing assignments, some of which are aimed primarily at helping the student learn to read philosophy properly, and some of which are aimed primarily at helping him write it. In addition, the quality of a student's final paper seems to be directly proportional to the amount of interaction that the student has with someone during the earlier stages of the paper's development."

Stephen A. O'Connell, a lecturer in the department of economics, praises Benoit for helping him "develop a coherent structure" for his course on the debt crisis. Christine M. Bachen, an assistant professor in the Annenberg School of Communications, commends WATU: "Its very existence is a reminder to faculty that successful command of material includes the ability to communicate that subject matter well, and that evaluations of students' work must include a review of how competently the student presented his/her knowledge." She explains that she has always provided explicit critiques of students' writing and that WATU encourages and trains graduate students to do so as well.

A. John Graham, chair of classics, commends WATU for strengthening his department's translation courses. He says that in smaller courses writing fellows make it possible to require drafts and rewriting with personal guidance, and in larger courses "the presence of WATU assistants has been the crucial factor making it possible for our thinly-stretched faculty and regular teaching assistants to give genuinely personal attention to students while still requiring serious written exercises. . . . " He also notes that his department's graduate students have gained added financial support and experience that help prepare them for academic appointments. In sum, he views WATU as "an extraordinarily cost-effective program," making an impact on the overall quality of teaching and of written work in his department's courses, as well as on the graduate students participating in the program.

Finally, N. Sivin, a professor of Chinese culture and of the history of science writes, "To my mind there is no other program at the university that does as much for the basic liberal component of education. . . . Seven or eight years ago I felt that my work on writing in both undergraduate and graduate courses was not accomplishing much, since it was not reinforced by a great deal of similar effort in other courses. The Writing Across the University program has changed that dramatically."

These reponses support the general belief in the quality and value of Writing across the University. This program is young, and it is still being defined. Even so, it is already recognized as important to the university. It has a philosophy and structure appropriate to its purposes. At this point, however, it seems to have two primary weaknesses. First, it has a critical instability because it does not have a regular source of funding, preferably one within the university. Second, simply because it is ambitious and at the same time economical, it does not yet have a solid training program. The director, the chair, and university administrators are working to find continuing funding, as we have seen, and training is also receiving attention.

In some ways, the source of the program's strengths may also be the source of its weaknesses. It is staffed by graduate students—working in various disciplines themselves. Because they know particular fields of study, they can be especially helpful to the faculty and students in affiliated courses. Because they do not need full-time employment, they can take on unusual and varying assignments. But these advantages also have a negative effect: a new program staffed by graduate students from many disciplines does not have a single and natural source of funding. Further, these graduate students are taking on new assignments that add to their regular load and their primary academic interests. Though writing is integral to their graduate study and to their professional careers, there are sharp limits on the time they can invest in training and perhaps also in their work in the program. One faculty member, troubled by the inadequacies of the training program, says that "TAs are learning about writing just the way they have for years, without benefit of the wisdom and expertise of those now working in composition as a profession." Kuriloff recognizes the need for a stronger training program, and she is, in fact, involving colleagues from the Graduate School of Education in that program.

Writing across the University, then, faces important challenges, but if it can meet them, it could become a solid and enduring program. We might take a proper note of optimism from Robert Lucid, the chair who imagined the program and saw it emerge into its present form. Lucid views the quality of instruction and the effect on students as imponderable. He's willing to settle, he said, "for raising the consciousness of faculty and graduate students." And he added that he can already see the program's effect on the structure of the school and on the attitude of faculty members and graduate students.

Freshman English Seminars

Like Writing across the University, the freshman seminars offered through the English department depend on graduate students and belong to a voluntary program. These seminars, however, gain stability in two ways: they are an enduring part of the English department's undergraduate curriculum and, at the same time, an element in a much broader Freshman Seminar Program. To understand and assess the freshman seminars, we need first to view them in the context of this larger program.

The freshman English seminars form two-thirds of Penn's Freshman Seminar Program, which the university describes in this way:

> The Freshman Seminar Program is designed to initiate freshmen into the University's approach to learning by providing them with the opportunity to work closely and in a small group setting with a teacher who is dedicated to a discipline. The freshman year should be a year of exploration. It should be a time to discover the University, to discover new disciplines and interests, and most of all to discover new things about oneself. (*Freshman Seminar Program, 1984-85* 2)

With enrollments limited to seventeen (and held to an average of fifteen in English), the program brings students close to their teachers and their peers. It allows the interaction that Penn considers essential for "helping students make the transition from a high school to a university that stresses the need for independent and critical thinking" (2). Seminars range from introductory English courses through specialized courses taught by faculty members of the graduate and professional schools. Offerings for fall 1984 included Philosophical Problems in Modern Biology (Sol Goodgal, professor of microbiology in the School of Medicine), The Cosmic Perspective (Benjamin S. P. Shen, Reese W. Flower Professor of Astronomy and Astrophysics), Hindu India: A Different View of the World (Ludo Rocher, W. Norman Brown Professor of South Asia Regional Studies), and Introduction to Jewish Law (Barry L. Eichler, associate professor of Assyriology).

As part of the Freshman Seminar Program, the English seminars are elective. The composition requirement was discontinued in 1971. Joel Conarroe, then director of freshman English, presented these seminars as a means of satisfying the humanities requirements—and enrollments went up. With composition required, students wanted and found means to be exempted. With freshman English an elective, an attractive one, they became interested in enrolling. Even now, only the Wharton School and the School of Nursing require students to take these seminars, yet enrollments remain very high. Some twenty-two hundred students enter Penn each year, and over two thousand enroll in freshman English seminars. Students in the College of Arts and Sciences must take three courses in the humanities, three in the social sciences, and three in the natural sciences. Only one in each field must be an upper-division course. Penn has a de facto core curriculum for some students: in their first year, pre-med students take language, math, chemistry, and a freshman seminar; entering Wharton students take economics, math, business, and a freshman seminar. Only in the freshman seminars do they have freedom to choose courses to meet their particular interests.

In addition to being elective, these seminars are dramatically varied. Though all sections emphasize writing, they are based on literary genres or themes. They are taught under these rubrics: 01, The Craft of Prose; 03, The Narrative; 04, The Experience of Poetry; 05, The Art of the Novel; 06, Short Fiction; 07, The Epic Tradition; 08, Drama; 09, Literature and Human Values; and 10, Creative Writing. Courses for fall 1984 included Medieval Stories and Storytellers: Or, The Lighter Side of "The Dark Ages," Evolutionary Fictions, The Sixties and the Myth of the Sixties, Realism and the American Novel, Shakespeare's History Plays, Women Writers as Mythmakers, and The Fortunate Fall: The Changing Role of the Artist.

As I have said, almost all the seminars are taught by graduate students, who, trained and supervised, may present courses of their own design. Thus, the graduate students, like the distinguished professors, are creating courses based on their special interests and expertise. They are, like the freshmen, choosing courses that especially appeal to them. Those I spoke with find these common elements in their seminars: drafts, conferences, collaborative learning (small-group discussions of drafts), and the amount of writing required. The teaching fellows receive these guidelines for written assignments:

> During the course of the semester each student should expect to write an average of 750-1,000 words per week. Assignments should be frequent and diverse, consisting of both formal writing (papers, essay exams, etc.) and informal, ungraded writing (journals, rough drafts, in-class exercises, and so forth). Students should receive at least four grades on a minimum of twenty pages of formal writing.

The guidelines describe the purpose of the course in this way:

> Each course is designed to improve and expand the student's ability to read critically, understand and discuss the genre or theme with which the course deals, and write better. Special emphasis is put on the writing of frequent critical and expository essays in order to develop writing skills. Thus all literature courses are also composition courses. (Information for Teaching Fellows 1)

The graduate students teaching freshman seminars are supervised by David Espey, coordinator of freshman English and graduate studies. Espey came to the position from the office of the associate dean for undergraduate studies, and he maintains some connection with that office. Under a grant from the Exxon Foundation, he initiated Undergraduate Essay Awards as well. He holds an appointment similar to Kuriloff's, teaching half-time and administering the program. Through both assignments, he helps the graduate students draw together their joint responsibilities for study and teaching. In addition to guiding those teaching for him, he sits on the department's graduate committee and assists in the graduate course required of all new teaching assistants.

That course, now designated as English 800, shows students the intellectual and pedagogical connections between their graduate study of literature and their teaching of literature and composition. It was carefully crafted by Peter Conn and Humphrey Tonkin, who participated in a program at Beaver College the summer before they taught it for the first time, in the fall of 1981. As Peter Conn reports in "Combining Literature and Composition: English 886" (*ADE Bulletin* 72 [1982]: 4-6), the graduate course for first-year TAs parallels the freshman seminars they are teaching. Conn says, "I have been unable to come up with a clever image for this arrangement. I keep thinking of the Starship *Enterprise*, periodically sending out and then receiving back its smaller landing craft" (4). The 800-level course is a demanding graduate-level course on a particular topic: Conn taught a course on American fiction and Tonkin, a course focused on allegory; in the fall of 1984, Vicki Mahaffey taught a course on modernism. The faculty member and graduate students together design a scaled-down version of the course for freshmen, taught simultaneously in the Freshman Seminar Progam.

During the term, David Espey meets with the graduate class regularly to discuss the theory and practice of composition. In the fall of 1984, he presented workshops on these topics: leading a discussion, commenting on students' writing, collaborative learning, revision, and teaching writing. In addition, graduate students read current materials on composition and also made presentations to their colleagues.

I discussed English 800 with Vicki Mahaffey, an assistant professor of English who taught the course in the fall of 1984, and with a small group of current teaching fellows. The graduate students said that the course varies a good deal from term to term, depending on its subject and the teacher's degree of interest in composition, but that they found it challenging and extremely useful. They praised it not only for the help it gave them in designing and teaching their classes but also for its value to their studies. Some described it as one of the best graduate courses at Penn.

Vicki Mahaffey, who argued strongly against separating composition and literature, said that many new graduate students lack precision and care in their own reading and writing. She feels that they should have training in logic and rhetorical techniques before they are introduced to composition theory. The most practical elements of their work in composition, then, seem most useful to her. In her course, she focused on the connections between modernism and the classroom. Her course description begins in this way:

> Modernism is an inherently pedagogical movement; its aims, like those
> of the New Criticism it spawned and outlived, intersect with those of the
> classroom in interesting ways: it seeks to provoke and inspire a greater
> awareness of the way that meaning is produced, while giving equal em-
> phasis to the view that meaning is a fictive construct that can never fully
> account for the complexity of experience. The Modernist writers take as
> their subject the seductiveness and elusiveness of meaning, the power
> and inefficacy of language to express or convey it.

While she was teaching this course, she and her students were also teaching
English 9, Mutations of Identity.

During the term, the English 800 instructor visits her students in their
classrooms. After completing that course, they are assigned faculty advisers,
who visit their classes twice a semester. The question, of course, is whether
or not a program as ambitious as this can guarantee consistency from
classroom to classroom. The question applies both when teaching fellows
prepare their courses and when they are teaching them. David Espey pointed out that in their first year graduate students serve as teaching apprentices in large courses; only in their second do they take English 800 and teach
freshman seminars, under extremely close supervision and with perhaps unusual support (through English 800). He feels strongly that what might be
lost in allowing trained fellows to design their own courses is certainly gained
in morale. The graduate students also pointed out that they share and trade
assignments and ideas, often through study groups, and that they participate in the colloquiums sponsored by WATU. They feel that they have
considerable freedom but that help is available.

Perhaps equally important, in the fall of 1984 freshman English supported
everyone in the department's graduate program. After completing a teaching apprenticeship in the first year, graduate students serve as teaching
fellows, teaching one course each term and receiving approximately $6,000
per year, in addition to tuition remission of more than $10,000. In their
fourth and following years, graduate students serve as lecturers, teaching
two courses in the fall, at $2,600 per course. Approximately twenty fellow-
ships were also awarded to advanced graduate students in 1984–85. After the
fourth year, students pay a dissertation fee of $800 per semester. Most are in
the program for seven or eight years, with continuing support. In 1984-85, instead of going outside Penn to hire adjuncts, the department supported
graduate students in other fields: American civilization, comparative literature, education, folklore, and communications. About a dozen graduate
students from other departments received support.

The freshman seminars are, obviously, an instance of what composition
specialists now commonly question as traditional literature—and composition—classes. Do they work? As Robert Lucid said of Writing across the
University, it's hard to prove success. But the program encourages the
graduate students to join literature and composition in their own work and
in their classes, and it draws strong voluntary participation from both the

students and the teaching fellows. Penn has a philosophy and purpose capable of sustaining such a program, and it offers the right environment. The primary issue here is economy: given this number of sections, this number of graduate students, how can a program director develop control and ensure consistency from classroom to classroom? English 800 is an important means of helping students discover the connections between their study and their teaching, and this course provides a sound conceptual base for the freshman seminars. Perhaps new strategies can be developed for extending the training program to provide continuing support and instruction for the TAs. They are already invited to participate in the colloquiums sponsored by WATU. Perhaps some method can also be devised for pulling individual courses closer together within designated categories, which might be thematic or structural, focused on literature or on composition.

Overall, however, the freshman English seminars—and Writing across the University—seem strikingly appropriate for this university. These two programs show how academic courses and programs can be tailored to individual campuses. Both the freshman seminars and WATU reflect the traditions, commitments, and interests of Penn, and both seem to hold positions of respect. If I see a single need joining them, it is the need to coordinate their efforts. As WATU advances in age and, ideally, in wealth, the two directors may find reason and procedures for linking their programs more closely. And they should take courage: the questions before them—how to join research and teaching, how to allow freedom while maintaining control—are central not only to their own programs but also to the profession.

Agenda for Campus Visit

Monday, 22 April 1985

   5:00   Peshe Kuriloff, coordinator of the Writing Center and Writing across the Curriculum

Tuesday, 23 April 1985

   9:00   Thomas Ehrlich, provost

 10:00   John Benoit and Julie Dobrow, WATU senior fellows

 12:00   Robert Lucid, chair of the English department

  1:30   David Espey, coordinator of freshman English and graduate studies

  3:00   Linda Brodkey, assistant professor of education and WATU consultant

  4:00   Vicki Mahaffey, assistant professor of English

  8:00   Elaine Maimon, consultant (by telephone)

Wednesday, 24 April 1985

 11:30   Joel Conarroe, dean of the School of Arts and Sciences

12:00   David Espey; Peshe Kuriloff; and Doug Buchholz, Cindy
        Giddle, Carol Schilling, and Susan Yager, teaching fellows

1:00   Carol Schilling, WATU senior fellow

(Additional phone conversation with Elaine Maimon, 10 June 1985)

Materials Reviewed

University Planning

Fitts, Donald D., acting dean, Faculty of Arts and Sciences. Memo to Peter Conn, associate dean for undergraduate studies, et al., 7 Mar. 1983: strategic planning.

Hackney, Sheldon, "Building Connections: A Report from the President to the University Community." *Almanac Supplement* 25 Oct. 1983: I-VIII.

———. "President's Report 1983." *Almanac* 15 Nov. 1983: 1-12.

Writing across the University

Colloquium Series: schedule.

Courses Affiliated with Writing across the University, Spring 1985.

Faculty Report: form.

Fellows' reports.

Historical Summary of Financial Support, 19 Apr. 1985.

Kuriloff, Peshe, and Robert F. Lucid. Letter to affiliated faculty and friends of Writing across the University, 25 Feb. 1985.

Letters of support from affiliated faculty.

An Optimum Budget for FY 1986.

Proposal to the AT&T Foundation, Dec. 1984.

Responsibilities of a Writing Fellow.

Responsibilities of a Writing Fellow: Training.

Sample Evaluation Form.

Sample Letter to Student.

Writing across the University 1984-85.

Writing across the University: Program Description, Fall 1985.

University Writing Center and Writing Lab

Kuriloff, Peshe. Memo to WATU fellows and affiliated faculty, 14 Feb. 1985: Writing Lab in Bennett Hall.

University Writing Center: Guidelines.

University Writing Lab: Guidelines.

We'll Read What You Write.

Writing Center Evaluations, Spring 1985: form.

Writing Center staff. Memo to faculty and teaching assistants in writing intensive courses: acknowledgments page.

Freshman English

Freshman English, 1984-85.
Freshman Seminar Program, 1984-85.
Information for Teaching Fellows.
Sample syllabi.

Graduate Course for TAs

Conn, Peter. "Combining Literature and Composition: English 886." *ADE Bulletin* 72 (1982): 4-6.
Course syllabi, materials, or descriptions: David Espey, Fall 1984; Vicki Mahaffey, Fall 1984; W. Steiner, Fall 1983; Peter Conn, Fall 1982; Humphrey Tonkin, Fall 1981.

CHAPTER 10

Harvard University

THE EXPOSITORY WRITING Program at Harvard is an independent writing program, working effectively outside an English department. With a temporary staff, the program holds its place in the university primarily through the strong presence of its director, Richard Marius. Marius reports to the associate dean for undergraduate education, Steven Ozment, who appoints and chairs the standing faculty committee that oversees the program. Having been named director, Marius is trusted in his position and, for the most part, allowed to manage his program as he thinks best. He himself is drawn into the affairs of the university through his teaching, committee service, and appearances before alumni and prospective students.

The program depends on Marius to give it not only shelter but character. He informs the program through the appointments he makes and through the freedom he in turn gives those he hires—practicing writers, publishing fiction, poetry, and expository prose. They shape their courses, by section and type (or "sort"), working within the guidelines and influenced by the philosophy advanced by their director. Marius offers leadership and support, and he is himself very much present in the program. At the same time, he trusts and depends on those he has hired. As a result, the continuing full-time instructors ("preceptors") have taken on some administrative responsibility for the program.

In an independent program shaped definitively by its director and staff, hiring is critical. The initial decision to appoint Marius and his basic decision to hire writers have determined the program's character. And the current hiring process reflects the program's relation to the university as well as its own administrative structure: the Standing Committee on Expository Writing holds final authority for making full-time appointments, and the preceptors now influence recommendations. While we need, then, to focus on these hiring decisions and the mechanisms and forces for making them, we must also place them in their historical context. Some early decisions on hiring at Harvard have influenced the fate of rhetoric and composition in American universities, and a discussion of the current program has to take those decisions into account.

The story, as told by James J. Murphy, is as follows: Francis James Child accepted the Boylston Professorship at Harvard in 1851, bringing to the position "a background in German scholarship acquired at Göttingen and especially an interest in criticism as opposed to composition, either oral or written" ("Rhetorical History" 4). Child was offered a professorship at Johns Hopkins in 1876, but he declined, preferring to stay at Harvard with a new title, Professor of English. He was replaced as Boylston Professor by Adams Sherman Hill, who held the position from 1876 until 1904. As Murphy explains:

> During that quarter century Harvard established a new department of English, and the old training in oratory gradually disappeared as class sizes mushroomed and "courses" under the "elective" system replaced the old concept of a single curriculum for all students. Thus the term "composition" at Harvard came to mean only written composition, and the term "rhetoric" was narrowed to mean only oral composition. . . . By the 1890s, . . . a special committee of overseers at Harvard recommended that even written composition should be relegated to high schools. (4-5)

By separating rhetoric from literature and composition from rhetoric and then assigning composition to the schools, Harvard contributed to what has been seen as the decline of composition. These actions and their effects on teaching and research are well chronicled by Murphy, as well as by Albert R. Kitzhaber, Arthur N. Applebee, Donald C. Stewart, and, recently, Anne Ruggles Gere. Here we trace more narrowly the fate of composition—or writing—at Harvard.

As Marius explained to me, Harvard's required composition course has gone through several incarnations. In the late nineteenth century, Charles William Eliot, then the university's president, was disturbed because students couldn't write, and he decided they should be required to take a writing course. The course established in 1872, English A, endured until World War II. It was taught by instructors of various ranks, for English professors stopped teaching it early on. After World War II, the course moved into general education, where it remained until the early 1970s. "Gen Ed A" was ordinarily directed by a young member of the English faculty, someone holding the position for a year or two while struggling for tenure. About 1974, the course became part of an independent program, Expository Writing. The requirement was tightened, no exemptions to "Expos" being allowed. At the same time, however, the program "fell into administrative chaos." The title of director went to the associate dean for undergraduate education, but the program was managed by a committee and an assistant to the director. When the new core curriculum was established, the dean decided that a senior faculty member should direct the writing program. In June 1977, Harvard advertised for such a person.

Marius was teaching history at the University of Tennessee at the time. He had earned a BS in journalism at Tennessee and an MA and a PhD in history from Yale. While he was at Yale, he had edited a journal. Since then, he had been writing, and he had been teaching his history courses "as writing courses," his students producing eight-page papers every other week. Marius gained an interview—and the appointment. Reportedly, the hiring committee had suspected that a composition specialist might not succeed politically at Harvard, and some members of the committee had been skeptical of an English professor's ability to reach across the university. As a historian, as well as a novelist and journalist, Marius had published in several fields. He fit the concept of the core curriculum: writing should not be restricted to the English department.

Marius was named director and appointed senior lecturer in expository writing. When he arrived at Harvard, the standing committee, which had been making day-to-day decisions, gradually withdrew from administering the program. During his first year as director, Marius observed what was happening throughout the program. He visited forty-three classes in the first two months, and he started holding staff meetings. He began hiring writers to teach ("not just those with goodwill"), and he dismissed some instructors—or saw them resign.

The changes he proposed in one of the courses subjected him to vigorous attack from the *Harvard Crimson* and other sources, but Derek Bok, Harvard's president, invited Marius to dinner and "always greeted [him] with great public warmth" (Marius, letter to the author, 20 June 1985). Marius held his ground silently, finally earning a *Crimson* caricature of him singing, "The record shows I took the blows and did it MY WAAAAAAAY" (quoted by Marius in the letter cited above). The onslaught, Marius said, had more to do with establishing the program than did anything else that happened in its early years.

Now, according to Steven Ozment, associate dean for undergraduate education, "there's not a healthier program [on campus], none more respected by the administration and faculty." Ozment sees Marius as "an eloquent and dynamic advocate" for a program "that is well thought out and that works." At Harvard, Ozment explained, the Expos teacher is one of the closest advisers students have, someone who is sought out over the years. "When [Marius] came, the program was in shambles; now it's respected. . . . Everyone agrees he's doing a marvelous job: he's a strong administrator, . . . and he's getting green lights everywhere." But while Marius's independence earns respect, Ozment reported, there is some concern that Expos may be a world unto itself.

According to Marius, Harvard sees him "as a strange zebra on a horse farm." One of perhaps ten senior lecturers on the faculty of arts and sciences, he holds a half-time administrative and half-time faculty position that continues without limitation of time. With his appointment in expository writing, he has taught in the English department, offering a popular seminar on teaching expository writing. In 1984-85, the question was raised whether he could direct graduate work. To do so, he took an added appointment as senior lecturer in English, but he kept the program separate from the English department. Marius explained that he is "not itching to teach something else" or to see the program's structure or departmental status changed. But he would like to become a professor of expository writing; such an appointment would mean that he and his program had been taken in, and he would like to see the various writing programs on campus united.

Marius recognizes how largely the program now depends on him, and he's not sure anyone else could direct the program as he has created it. "That's a real failure," he said, adding that no other program at Harvard relies so heavily on any one person. Marius has given his program credibility because he fits in politically. He serves on the Committee on Undergraduate Education ("to integrate him as an individual into the community," Ozment explained), and he often represents Harvard in meetings with alumni and prospective students. Yet neither his status nor the program's reflects merely a general regard for writing programs. Representing and trusting his staff, Marius has won respect for the Expository Writing Program and given it a distinctive character. He speculates that if he were to leave, the program would become entirely different within two years.

The mechanism that joins the program to the university is very simple: Marius reports to the associate dean for undergraduate education and serves on the standing committee with final responsibility for hiring and general advisory duties for the program. This faculty committee, which helped manage the program before Marius came, now seems to function primarily as a hiring committee. Though part-time appointments are made within the program, full-time appointments follow this procedure: Marius and his staffing committee screen applications, interview large numbers of candidates, and advance a list (perhaps eight to ten candidates for one position) to the standing committee. This committee, together with one or two of the program's staff, conducts final interviews and makes decisions on appointment. Marius would like to see the standing committee become involved in the program's daily affairs: he would like committee members to attend staff meetings and to sit in on classes. Their contacts with the program remain informal now, with committee members occasionally meeting with preceptors or teaching assistants over lunch.

It is important that the standing committee supports Marius in his basic decision about the type of people who should be teaching expository writing. As soon as Marius took office, he began looking for writers to teach writing. Several practices follow from that decision and the way he implements it. Marius finds passionate and energetic people committed to writing and to teaching writing, and he influences hiring decisions. Until recently, Marius made all his program's recommendations on hiring; even now, he influences his staffing committee, which gives him final authority, and he has a vote on the standing committee. As a result, many of his teachers are, as one of them observed, "not too unlike him—energetic, definite." Marius himself describes this staff as "young, vigorous, intelligent, aggressive, and tremendously devoted to teaching." Further, these instructors bring their own experience and insight to the teaching of the craft they themselves practice. The process of writing, then, is a common, daily experience for those who talk to students about that process. Finally, the staff have a strong sense of shared identity: they are a community of writers, regularly discussing their own work, and a community of writing instructors, committed to the art that they teach.

Marius's relationship to his staff and his attitude toward their work can be seen in this excerpt from his Informal Notes for Teachers of Expository Writing in Harvard College, 1983:

> We are performing the most important educational task at Harvard. What we do becomes a foundation for what everyone else here does. We should be teaching our students not merely how to put words on paper or where the commas go; we should be teaching them how to think and how to imagine and how to shape and design the mental universe that they will inhabit all the rest of their lives. The evaluations they write of their experience in the course show that most of them appreciate what we do for them, and that appreciation is a great reward in its own right. But perhaps the best part of the job is that when we do it well, we become more vividly alive ourselves. You are part of a devoted and splendid staff. And I hope that you will find the experience of teaching here one of the best things that ever happened to you. (68)

These Informal Notes—sixty-eight pages of direction, encouragement, and advice—help define the courses the staff will be teaching and also help shape the community they are going to participate in. The designation "informal" suggests that the program is still taking shape and that the responsibility for it lies with the teachers, as well as the director. Marius does not dictate to his people. Instead, he chooses them carefully, then trusts and encourages them. He stays in close touch with them: he is in and out of his office, busy but present and available; he holds regular staff meetings; he visits classes; he reviews evaluations. An energetic director, he welcomes teachers who can demonstrate their passionate commitment to language with vitality and imagination.

The staff for 1984–85 included ten full-time preceptors, a special assistant to the director, thirty-five part-time teaching assistants, and four teaching fellows (the only graduate students on the teaching staff). In addition, the program was supported by an administrative assistant and a secretary. Those teaching part-time were earning $4,000 for each section they taught, with a maximum of four sections during the year. An experienced preceptor was earning $21,900, the pay having been raised substantially each year since Marius began directing the program.

Because of the director's administrative style and his confidence in his staff, a second layer of administration has developed in the Expos program. Marius is a leader, effective through personal force and intensity more than through detailed program management. He has given his teachers responsibility for their classes, and those continuing in the program have taken on some responsibility for managing it. The core of preceptors, full-time and experienced teachers, assumed that responsibility several years ago through what they describe as "a revolt of the colonels." This was "the best-natured revolt" Marius has ever seen: the preceptors wanted administrative roles that would strengthen their credentials. Until then, Marius had made all recommendations on hiring. Now a preceptor, William Corbett, chairs a staffing committee that advances recommendations for full-time appointments to the standing committee. During 1984–85 an evaluation committee directed a systematic and thorough review of the program and of each teacher's performance. The preceptors meet regularly with Marius to consider the business of the program, including student evaluations, classroom visits, teaching assignments, and reappointment. They also work with new and part-time teachers, grouped according to "sorts," to plan and discuss classes. The preceptors' role in hiring, planning, and evaluation is useful both to them, as a form of administrative experience, and to the program.

The preceptors' involvement clearly strengthens the program. Their successful effort to take on more responsibility suggests both their willingness to become involved and Marius's attention to them. The preceptors give new and part-time instructors access to the wisdom and the plans they have for teaching expository writing. In this way, the teaching staff not only shape individual sections but also help ensure consistency from section to section and sort to sort.

When I visited the program, two instructors were playing special administrative roles. As special assistant to the director, Elizabeth Buckley was tutoring students who needed added help, observing classes, serving on the staffing and evaluation committees, and offering other assistance. Lowry Pei, de facto assistant director before "the revolt," was handling scheduling and enrollments, keeping records on transfers and failures, assigning classrooms and offices, and advising on grades. He was also observing classes (by then having visited more than fifty) and serving on the staffing and evaluation committees. A preceptor, Pei taught one class each term. (As a reminder that this report describes programs as they existed in one academic year, 1984–85, let me explain that in the fall of 1985 Lowry Pei accepted an appointment as director of writing at Simmons College.)

The Expository Writing Program offers six sorts of the required one-semester writing course: Expository Writing 11, Literature; Expository Writing 12, History; Expository Writing 15, Science; Expository Writing 16, Social Studies; Expository Writing 17, Theory and Practice of Writing; and Expository Writing 18, Style and Device in Literary Creation. All entering freshmen, 1,600 to 1,650 each year, must take this course. By a computer sort, the class is assigned to take expository writing in either the fall or the spring. The preceptors then place students in sections of fifteen, with necessary changes being made or supervised—for a number of years—by

Lowry Pei. Approximately 110 sections are offered each year, in nearly equal numbers fall and spring semesters. In addition, all transfer students are required to take the course if they cannot present at least twenty pages of writing judged worthy of an A at Harvard; approximately half of the fifty to seventy-five students who transfer each year are held for the course. Classes meet for one hour twice a week, and all students are required to confer with their instructors at least three times during the term.

We can see how Marius views expository writing by turning to his Informal Notes, now in their third edition. Here Marius lays aside assumptions that Expos—and other freshman writing courses—can be taught by anyone with common sense and a handbook. Such assumptions "relegated the teaching of writing to the basement of academe": "If anybody could teach writing without preparation for the job, the job itself must be mindless and the people doing it academic drones put to work doing something no one else would do. A corollary was that students who took a writing course were learning something they should have learned in high school." He continues:

> If anybody who walked reasonably erect could teach writing, the job lost any academic respectability and the people taking the course were made to feel that it was some vague punishment inflicted on them for various unspecified sins. Since every Harvard freshman is required to take Expository Writing, this mentality made it seem that our first task was to chastise these students and put them in their place—a lowly one—and to let them know that, although they had been good enough to get into Harvard, the faculty was not especially impressed by their achievements nor delighted by their presence. I have always believed that the primary function of a writing course is to teach students how to observe sharply and to think clearly. (1)

Marius describes the course objectives by first explaining what they are not: "Our job is not to teach students merely to write an essay that is grammatically correct and clear enough to be understood by any literate person after one or two readings" (4). Denying that correctness is the measure of good writing, he describes "customary patterns of grammar and punctuation" as a means of helping readers "not only to absorb information but to feel comfortable while doing so" (5). And he emphasizes that "the major weight of our course lies in rhetoric rather than grammar" (6). Finally, he asks questions about topics, evidence, style, and form: "These and countless other questions are enough to occupy us during every session of our course and on for a lifetime of writing. They are the problems real writers have to solve in a real world. They require patient, dedicated, unending reflection, and they should be the foundation of this course" (6).

Marius describes the types of writing appropriate to the course: summary, inference, analysis, narration, argument, comparison. And he offers a ten-point (eleven-page) definition of the essay, "a written prose argument that we should do something or that we should believe something," "usually short enough to be read in one sitting" (12). The definition focuses on the characteristics of a good essay, which, among other things, "gets to the point quickly" (12), "dares something" (15), and "remains focused throughout on the promise the writer makes to readers in the beginning" (21). Continuing, Marius discusses audience, tone, the writing process, and practical matters having to do with the classroom and the program. These "informal notes," together with the preceptors' meetings for instructors teaching each of the sorts, help to ensure that all the sections have common elements.

Within this set of principles and guidelines, the sorts differ according to the focus and set of strategies appropriate to each. The distinctive elements of an individual sort can be seen, for example, in syllabi for Expos 18, Style and Device in Literary Creation. In this course, students read, analyze, and write short stories and other forms of prose. They might read selections from the *Norton Anthology of Short Fiction*, edited by R. V. Cassill, and write essays or exercises on certain features of these stories: beginnings or endings, for example, or narration or point of view. At the same time, they will be completing exercises in fiction writing and writing short stories. They may produce their critical essays and stories in discrete steps that emphasize the stages of planning, drafting, and revising work. One instructor's syllabus includes this caution: "Every way of analyzing the writing process into stages is a fiction; to some extent it is bound to be arbitrary, or a reflection of the person doing the analyzing. I don't offer this version as dogma. What is not fiction, however, is that writing *is* a process over time, not just the creation of one draft in one pass" (syllabus prepared by Pei, Spring 1985).

If students have problems in Expos classes, they are tutored by other Expos instructors. During 1984-85, the tutors were Elizabeth Buckley and Martha Wintner. They saw students by appointment, often weekly. Wintner, who saw fourteen students fall semester and eight in the spring, explained that the writers she met with most often had problems in brainstorming and organizing a topic. They needed to learn what constitutes a paragraph, how to move sentences around to give a paper coherence. She saw these students, as Mina Shaughnessy said, developing an idea, rather than presenting a developed idea. They also had some problems with grammar and mechanics, particularly punctuation.

Students who fail the course have been held for an additional semester, Expos 14 HF, and awarded course credit only after they satisfactorily complete that term's work. This course is being discontinued, however, and a preliminary course, Expos 5, introduced. At the time of this study, the remedial course was being proposed as a full-credit, pass/fail course, and two sections were planned for 1985-86, one for native and one for nonnative speakers.

In addition to the required writing courses, an advanced course, Expos 2, is offered as an elective. It was available to sixty students in 1984-85, though eighty-five wanted to register for it. Because of budgetary limits, the number was going to be reduced to thirty the next year, though Marius expected as many as one hundred to want the course.

These writing courses are supported and supplemented by the work of the Writing Center, directed in 1984–85 by a teaching assistant, Sheila Reindl, reporting to Marius. A staff of nine undergraduates work as peer tutors, holding mostly one-to-one one-hour conferences by appointment. They generally work ten to fifteen hours each week, and they spend two of those hours in supervision, listening to tapes, doing exercises, or role playing. The undergraduate tutors come from various fields of study, science majors outnumbering those in English. During 1984-85, they met with 550 students in 1,200 conference hours, most of them during fall semester. Forty percent of the conference time was spent with freshmen, half of them enrolled in Expos classes. Conference hours are supplemented by a Sunday-afternoon drop-in writers' studio, offering students a place to write and making two consultants available to them.

The Writing Center also offers workshops for professors and teaching fellows. The workshops focus on such topics as how to make assignments, how to make expectations clear, and how to respond to student writing. In addition, Writing Center tutors have met with faculty members teaching courses included in the core curriculum. They have conferred with more than eighty faculty members, asking what they want to see in student writing that they are not seeing.

The Writing Center presents itself as writer-centered, not product-centered and not service-centered. The peer tutors focus on the process of thinking about writing. They confront a wide range of problems, most having to do with organization and structure. They help students understand how to give shape to thought, to impose order on it, and they also help students deal with sentence-level problems and writer's block. The director expressed particular concern about the problems of students studying English as a second language.

The Writing Center uses careful selection and training procedures developed by the previous director, Larry Weinstein. Applicants must list their grades in all courses, submit writing samples, and complete several exercises designed to show how they would approach tutoring. "The best candidates," Reindl said, "understand there's a writer before them, someone who should be enabled to take charge of the situation." In 1984-85 the Writing Center staff interviewed 32 of 110 applicants. Conducted by the entire staff, the interview, like the training, has a prescribed form. Those hired spend some twenty-five to thirty hours in preparation that includes assigned reading, mock conferences, tapes, meetings, exercises, role playing, and discussion.

The teaching of writing is discussed throughout the Expository Writing Program. New teachers meet regularly to confer about such matters as how to make assignments and how to evaluate papers; those teaching the same sorts meet once a month; and all instructors attend a general staff meeting once a month. The conversations begun in these meetings are extended through correspondence and reports. As I went through office files, reading letters on classroom observations, memos to the staff, evaluations, comments on student essays, and the essays themselves, I was impressed with the openness and thoroughness of the discussions. Everyone seems engaged with ideas and with the idea of writing. The teachers show not only a commitment to writing but also a willingness to engage in dialogue and in relationships—that is, to build a community.

The classroom observations, for example, are generally two- to four-page letters addressed to the staff members observed. Often, these refer to previous classes or discussions of classroom performance, and apparently the written reports are followed by some discussion in person. Again, one has the sense of continuing engagement: these people are working together, and they are working to improve teaching and their students' writing.

Clearly, Marius rejoices in the talents and accomplishments of his staff, writing his compliments and praising them as developing or experienced teachers. True, his negative comments can also be direct: "You talk far too much. . . . Students don't pay attention. . . . The trick you are going to have to learn is to draw out of your students what you are trying to pour into them." But each letter seems clearly addressed to an individual staff member, the tone as well as the substance reflecting the particular teacher and his or her performance in the classroom. Criticisms are followed by suggestions—techniques for asking questions or imitation exercises that might be developed, for example—and, when necessary, substantial explanations of various principles for writing well, at the level of either the sentence or the complete essay. Everyone Marius addresses receives words of encouragement: "So you have to lead them a little more strongly while at the same time retaining your gentleness and geniality." These letters and my conversations with Marius suggest that he wants to support each of his teachers, to inspire excellence in the classroom and community within the program.

The attitude and effort of the director are reinforced by those of his assistants. For example, when a new staff member had difficulty commenting on her students' papers, Pei wrote her a five-page letter, enclosing a full set of his comments on a weak student's essays, explaining the rationale and some of the details of his remarks, then reflecting on the instructor's comments on the work of a poor student. Throughout, he supported her as a colleague. I understand that this instructor continues to serve on the staff. Marius told me that he would ordinarily rather reappoint than replace a current staff member, even if that person is relatively weak. He tries to help those he has hired become stronger, more confident, more effective teachers. When problems appear, Marius and his preceptors prefer to deal with them, not by dismissing the person involved, but by correcting them and thereby strengthening the teacher and the staff.

The most extensive—and the most impressive—evidence of this approach is in the complete self-evaluation of the program. I reviewed the forms for student, staff, and preceptor evaluation in 1984-85; I read through staff members' self-evaluations and supporting materials; and I read Pei's summary memo to the staff (Memo to All Teachers in Expos). That memo reports the committee's findings and discusses the principles and assumptions guiding their work.

Explaining how the committee handled the materials they received, Pei comments on their efforts to read and understand student evaluations in the context of the course taught: "Our job, we came to assume, was to figure out (if we could) how the students' reaction to a particular Expos section connected to the design of that course as reflected in the syllabus, the execution of it as reflected in the paper comments and assignments, the teacher's tone and assumptions as reflected in the self-evaluation"(2). He describes the committee's work as an effort "to find out where the action was in each teacher's encounter with the students—where the crucial communication took place. The division of labor between class, conferences, paper comments, and handouts is different for each teacher; [the committee] tried to understand this pattern for each" (4). He goes on to explain, "We did not try to judge these strategies relative to each other; the question was whether they worked for the students, and whether the teacher might be able to get the same result in an easier way (not that there is an easy way of teaching Expos—that much is clear)" (5).

Further, Pei observes:

> No doubt everyone reading this report will want to hear something about the overall quality of the program; frustratingly, one of our conclusions is that such a generalization might not be valid. Still, we found more reason for satisfaction than for dissatisfaction, more excitement over surprising excellence than over lurking troubles. Compared to the Expos of 1978, when I first came here, we are already off the charts—we as a group know so much better what to do and how to do it, and we are so much less a random collection of approaches, that there's hardly any point in comparison.

The committee drew the broad conclusion "that Expos still is more a collection of individuals, and less a set of six courses teaching the same things in alternate ways, than [they] might have thought or hoped when [they] began." They address problems of inconsistency in grading, which they view as inconsistency "in the meanings that teachers try to convey through grades," as well as inconsistency "in the amount of work demanded, the intellectual substance of the work demanded, and the amount that students feel they can learn from the work" (5-6).

To address the problems identified in the evaluation, the committee propose three types of related discussions: "about the definition of a sort or the entire program, about specific issues in the execution of our job, and about the individual issues each teacher faces personally." The committee had already written to all teachers evaluated and had also spoken to many of them about their work.

In summary, Pei describes "what Expos is when it works at its best":

> Perhaps the primary quality of the best Expos classes is that in them nearly everything (the students' papers or revisions, the comments on those papers, class discussions, conferences, handouts, assignment descriptions) is part of a dialogue between teacher and student about how the student's writing is developing. There is a strong sense of two-way communication, of teacher and student somehow becoming able to hear something close to what the other actually thinks. All the channels of communication . . . share this tone: that conversation, not prescription, is the ultimate point, though prescription may well be a way of making better conversation possible.

Pei explains that in these classes the syllabi show progression and design, conferences are prominent, the writing tasks "are real tasks," and high-level performance is expected. The point I consider most important appears in the midst of that series: "The comments on papers, whether long or short—many are long (250-750 words)—are well-written. Not only are they precise and subtle, they have voice, they may use metaphor or imagery in an idiosyncratic way, they take a tone toward the student which implies a knowledge of the person being addressed—in short, they are real writing. The same could be said of assignments and other handouts" (13-14).

Thus, the evaluation committee identify in the classroom exactly what I see in the program: a belief in language, an easy dependence on it as the medium for developing community and understanding. Writing is so natural for these teachers, such an essential element in all their negotiations, that they teach it automatically, through example as well as precept. Here, writing is necessarily taught as process, for it is not only the subject of instruction but also an important means of creating the course and the program itself.

When I asked Lowry Pei if I could see some student essays and his comments on them, he showed me a file of essays and offered me an eight-inch stack of comments he had written. Pei had marked each essay and also typed a page or two of comments on each one. His remarks usually moved from the general (overall evaluation, comparison with earlier drafts) to the specific (response to points the writer makes, comments on the line of reasoning and information presented or neglected, discussion of voice or style) and back to the general (degree of success, comparison with other papers, advice for revising this paper or writing another). Pei had commented not only on the student's writing but also on his own comments, explaining how the student's writing made him respond as he did. He often explained how the writer had created certain expectations and then succeeded or failed to meet them. He had read one paper three times, and he explained his response each time and his reasons for rereading. Pei's notes, clearly addressed to individual writers, were those of a sympathetic but critical reader who writes every day: "It's easy to say this as a reader, but it can be damned hard to make it happen as a writer. . . ."

From all that I've said, it's clear that I think Harvard's Expository Writing Program works exceptionally well, although I can't comment on how much students improve in these classes. I looked at essays written for Expos 16 and 18 (most of them six to eight pages, normally well structured and well written) and a few presented to one of the tutors (papers that of course display less accomplished writing and more flaws but that are nonetheless the work of bright students). I looked at these papers, however, not to judge the students' or the teachers' achievements but to learn what kind of writing is done in certain classes and how the teachers respond to it. Measuring students' progress and evaluating the accomplishments of any writing program still vex those of us called on to do so on our own campuses. More important, I found the Harvard program successful in these ways: it is based on the clearly formulated philosophy that writing should be taught by writers and that students in writing classes should learn "how to observe sharply and think clearly" (Marius, Informal Notes 1); it is directed by a forceful leader and recognized scholar committed to his teachers, to his program, and to writing; it is staffed by articulate, intelligent, and energetic writers committed to teaching; and it has been carefully evaluated by those responsible for teaching in it.

The most important questions that remain, then, concern the program's future. These center on the status of the instructors and the scope of the program itself. Marius is the only staff member who is not temporary, and some of his preceptors are nearing the limits of their eligibility. Further, the program is designed primarily for freshmen, and its advanced courses are being cut back just at a time when advanced writing and writing across the curriculum are receiving increased attention nationally.

Although in 1985 the issue of security was the less imminent problem, in that the preceptors with the greatest seniority had two years' eligibility remaining, it was even then the larger and more pressing of the two. Preceptors at Harvard can teach full-time for eight years; teaching assistants (those working part-time) can teach four, with the possibility of six in special circumstances. Although a category of senior preceptor does exist, no one in the program had yet earned such an appointment. (Elizabeth Buckley, a former preceptor, gained a position as special assistant to the director, but, unfortunately, the former director of the Writing Center had to be released when his eligibility ran out.)

One of the preceptors I spoke with said that the insecurity of the position was only then becoming a problem, with three staff members near the limit for reappointment. He showed concern both for the program and for his own career. "The university labors under the delusion . . . that there's a river of great teachers out there and all we need to do is divert some of them," he said. He explained that Expos 18 has become what it is because a core of great teachers has been together for years, talking about it and using one another's ideas. He believes strongly that this relationship and shared history help account for the excellence of the program. The theory, he said, is that there's some Platonic essence to a program that people can come in and do. Yet those who have taught Expos 18 have made it what it is, and it can't now be maintained by turning over a handbook to new instructors. He also thinks that the university may have to change some of its policies (to begin offering indefinitely renewable contracts, for example) if the program is to continue being what it is.

This experienced preceptor also considers status an issue for those holding temporary appointments. He believes they do feel marginal and generally unappreciated. On the other hand, some in this program find an advantage in being marginal rather than holding tenure-track appointments. As writers, they want the freedom they have in this program. But as the program becomes more professional and as the staff matures, this preceptor finds it harder to accept a marginal role.

As we spoke, I came to understand the close connection between the issue of temporary appointments and that of the evolution of a program. In principle, temporary appointments can be defended as a means of mounting ambitious programs, assuming that these are good appointments helping prepare people for secure positions. Such appointments do allow those with special skills and expertise, sometimes without normal academic credentials, to hold full-time university teaching positions. In practice, however, this system seems to change with time. The problem is not simply that in practice temporary people often are not treated well, though that is the issue that has generated most attention and concern. It is that, even in programs in which they are treated well, the status of temporary staff members changes over time. In fact, as they gain seniority and value in the program, they approach the limits of their eligibility. Here, chronology seems to matter as much as hierarchy. Having invested some years of their professional lives in a particular program, temporary instructors have helped to shape and define it, and as that program matures, it owes some of its identity to them. But does the program have some further obligation to them? If so, is it an obligation that cannot be honored? At some point in the development of the program and of the temporary staff members' careers, it would seem best to decide that at least some might stay on. They could do so, however, only under new terms of appointment, and the issue becomes whether or not those terms can be arranged.

The question is further complicated when those holding temporary appointments are writers, for they may very well practice and publish regularly without gaining academically acceptable credentials. I talked with several preceptors about their views on the role of writers teaching in a university program without regular faculty status. One feels strongly that writers serve as a corrective and as a reminder that writing demands talent. He argued that to be a writer is to be a thinker, which is to be a person. Since writing thus becomes the basis for society, "if you walk into a university and have to defend writing, that place is not a university." Then, he said, you begin talking about "composition" and attempt to earn recognition for it as a discipline, to have its legitimacy and authority accepted. Thus, he argued, my question about whether or not composition is an academic discipline is framed incorrectly: he wouldn't give tenure in composition and he doesn't conceive of composition as the business of writing teachers. Given the Germanic tradition of scholarship, we have gradually developed such a thing as academic writing, the particular kind required for a PhD. It makes sense for anyone who wants to work in the university to try to establish composition as a discipline. But "composition" is the wrong word. We need to talk about "writing" and let those who are writers teach it.

To provide a valuable lesson in perspective, let me offer here the views on preceptors' appointments expressed by Marius and by Donald Stone, a professor of French and a member of the standing committee. According to Stone, Marius could already be proposing that some preceptors be appointed as senior preceptors if it weren't for a Massachusetts ruling on retirement policies. Retirement is now mandatory only for fire fighters, police officers, and tenured professors. "Senior preceptors" are not included in the category of "professors," and so they are exempt from mandatory retirement. As a result, Marius explains, "Harvard has frozen all preceptorial appointments and all other teaching appointments not on the professorial level but carrying no limitation of time" (letter to the author, 20 June 1985). If this problem is corrected so that senior preceptors can be appointed or if, as Marius and Stone suggest, "a series of revolving five-year appointments" could be made (letter cited above), those who are now preceptors could continue teaching in the program. All recommendations for advancement or continuing appointment, and all decisions, would be based on merit, rather than on numbers. That is, the issue would not be how many candidates Marius was proposing for these appointments but, rather, how well qualified each candidate was.

These plans sound reasonable and fair: advancement or continuing appointment should not be automatic, certainly, but it should be possible. This situation points out the importance of communication and of honest self-assessment. People and programs need continually to be taking their own measure. Indeed, Marius confirmed, some of the current preceptors do have academically acceptable credentials. Some are regularly publishing their own writing, others publishing both creative writing and literary scholarship. This information came to me as a reminder that we need to be cautious in generalizing about the state of those holding temporary appointments.

The second issue, that of the program's responsibility to advanced students, is being addressed in two ways. First, the program's budget for 1985–86 was expected to reduce the number of advanced sections available. Again we face the issue of perspective, for while Marius described the limit on his budget as a cut, Ozment explained that the budget would increase by five to seven percent rather than continuing to increase by thirty to forty percent each year. The result, however, was that Marius expected to schedule fewer advanced sections than were offered in 1984–85—and fewer than student demand would bear. Ozment did say that he doesn't believe that the program's growth should be in the direction of Expos 2, primarily because advanced instruction should be offered in connection with individual departments. Both Ozment and Stone seem to doubt that the program's staff would be accepted as teachers for advanced levels. Here, then, a financial issue shades into a pedagogical one.

Second, new attention is being given to the instruction offered by graduate students working as teaching fellows. Because these students do most of the paper reading and grading, Ozment is encouraging Marius to prepare them to be teachers of writing. At the time of this study the first plans had been made: over the summer of 1985, Marius was to prepare a manual on assigning, reading, commenting on, and grading papers, and during the fall he would offer weekly lectures on topics such as writing and thinking, finding a topic, and the writing process. In this way, Ozment said, the Expository Writing Program would become more integrated into the Harvard community. This plan, of course, was economical, so once again there was some blending of financial and pedagogical issues.

Overall, then, it seems that the program may gradually affect more and more undergraduate instruction but that it will do so indirectly, through its director rather than through its staff. Within its own terms, the program seems likely to remain at or near its present size and to continue to develop through questioning and focused discussion. Given the program's separation from the rest of the university and the special character of its faculty, the staff itself will continue to be of central importance, for the program can maintain its vitality only through the presence, the creative energy, and the dedication of the director and the teachers. Donald Stone suggested to me that, given the autonomy of faculty and departments at Harvard, the program is severely limited in determining the university's attitude toward it, yet it can determine its attitude toward itself. Certainly, Richard Marius and his faculty can take pride in their accomplishment in creating a place, a community dedicated to writing and to teaching others to write.

Agenda for Campus Visit

Thursday, 25 April 1985

  8:30   Richard Marius, director of the Expository Writing Program

10:00   Sheila Reindl, director of the Writing Center

10:45   Martha Wintner, teaching assistant

11:15   Jay Boggis, teaching assistant

12:00   Steven Ozment, associate dean for undergraduate education

  1:30   Expository Writing 18, taught by Judith Cohen

2:00   Lowry Pei, preceptor

4:00   Richard Marius; Elizabeth Buckley; Sheila Reindl; Jeff Bradley, Judith Cohen, William Corbett, John de Cuevas, Sue Lonoff, Lowry Pei, John Perry, Nancy Piore, Linda Simon, preceptors

5:00   Judith Cohen, William Corbett, Lowry Pei, Nancy Piore

6:00   Richard Marius, Lowry Pei, Linda Simon

Friday, 26 April 1985

11:45   Elizabeth Buckley, Lowry Pei

Saturday, 27 April 1985

12:00   Richard Marius; Donald Stone, professor of French and member of the Standing Committee on Expository Writing

Materials Reviewed

The Expository Writing Program

Campbell, Colin. "Colleges Renew Emphasis on Writing Instruction." *New York Times* 25 Mar. 1985: A10.

Marius, Richard. Informal Notes for Teachers of Expository Writing in Harvard College, 1983.

Memos and agendas for staff meetings.

Pei, Lowry. Memo to Expos Teachers Generally, Fall 1984: general thoughts on what our program is up to and where it might go.

———. Some Other Remarks on Teaching Expos, c. 1981.

Expository Writing Courses

Draft course descriptions for Expos 16.

Essays presented to Martha Wintner for tutorial assistance.

Expository Writing Courses, 1984-85.

Sample comments on student essays.

Sample syllabi and assignments for Expos 16, 18, and 2.

Student essays for Expos 16 and 18.

The Writing Center

Application to Be a Writing Center Peer Consultant: form and sample essays.

Brochures and flyers.

How Can I Help My Students Write Better Papers? Workshops for Professors and Teaching Fellows.

Parts of a Conference at the Writing Center.

Evaluation and Review

Evaluation forms for students, staff, and preceptors, 1984-85.

Memos on teaching and performance in the program.

Pei, Lowry. Memo to All Teachers in Expos: The News till Now, Jan. 1985: a report on the work of the evaluation committee.
Quotations from Fall 1981 evaluations.
Self-review reports and materials for individual staff members.

Conclusion

W HILE I WOULD LIKE THE case studies to stand alone, a set of three placed against the backdrop of other AAU programs, I know I should try to articulate some of what I've seen in carrying out this study. I hesitate to make comparisons because comparisons lead toward judgments, and my aim has been not to discover which of these programs is best but to understand how writing programs work and how they suit their universities. I have assumed that students will learn to write in many kinds of classrooms and that the director's job is to ensure that teaching and learning occur in other than a random way. As a result, I have focused on program administration, considering the structures, the practices, and the leadership that might enable both teachers and students to perform well.

Of course, I visited Harvard, Penn, and North Carolina, Chapel Hill, because the programs there seemed very good: the directors' responses to my survey and interview questions, like the materials they sent me, suggested that these programs deserve notice. I was especially interested, however, because the programs are of distinctly different types. Each represents a major option in writing program administration today, yet each remains unique. Further, their directors have energy and imagination, and I saw very early that a study of these programs would become a study of academic leadership. Given my interests, I do not estimate the relative merits of the programs I visited. Rather, I compare them and place them in the context of other AAU writing programs in order to show what attempts are being made to secure a legitimate place for composition in the academy.

Here, I again take up the central elements of program administration presented in part 1. Attending first to the reality of change, I next consider administrative structures, program directors, faculty and teaching assistants, and course offerings. For each subject, I place the programs at Harvard, Penn, and North Carolina, Chapel Hill, side by side, and I also set them in relief against other programs studied. To do so, I use a few statistics and a few examples, and I suggest some of the issues being addressed in various areas. Following this anatomy of writing programs, I return to the larger issue of composition's status. To address it, I again look at each program visited, observing its relation to the English department, its fit within the university, and the form of its authority. This analysis necessarily takes us back and forth from program to program and up and down the scale of abstraction.

The programs at Harvard, Penn, and North Carolina, Chapel Hill—like many others—have changed dramatically in the past ten years. Recall that 36 of the 44 AAU writing programs responding to the survey have undergone major changes in the past ten years and nearly all the remaining 8 have changed in some ways or are now expecting important changes. The number of major changes peaked slightly in the late seventies but continued high into the eighties: Marius went to Harvard in 1978 and Lindemann to Chapel Hill in 1980; the Writing across the University Program that Kuriloff now directs at Penn was initiated in 1982. In AAU programs, the strongest forces for change were found within the faculty, students, and administration of local campuses or within composition, rhetoric, and related fields. On all three campuses visited, changes in the writing programs have been associated with broad curricular reviews and have depended on faculty and administrative support, as well as on leadership within the program. While these changes have been local matters, they have also occurred in a national context of attention to writing. On campuses across the country, writing programs have seen the need and the opportunity for change. Because programs are governed by their own circumstances, their responses have been various, though together they seem to form detectable patterns. Thus, the programs at Harvard, Penn, and North Carolina, Chapel Hill, have changed to serve their own campuses, but they have also been part of a larger phenomenon, helping to define the choices that can be made to improve the quality of writing programs across the country.

A basic choice is evident in responses to the first question on my written survey: "Does one academic unit offer or coordinate all instruction in English composition on your campus?" The answer was no for only 12 of the 41 campuses studied. The answer was yes for 29 campuses, including those I visited. Penn and North Carolina, Chapel Hill, were among the 20 (or two-thirds) in this category that named the English department or a program within it as the unit responsible for writing. Harvard was among the 9 naming other academic units, along with UCLA; Minnesota, Minneapolis and St. Paul; MIT; USC; California, San Diego; Yale; Clark; and Vanderbilt.

While the programs at both North Carolina, Chapel Hill, and Penn fit within the English department, the program at Chapel Hill is the more traditional embodiment of the type. It offers a three-semester introductory sequence, into which freshmen are placed according to their levels of proficiency. Three advanced writing courses are also available, along with an elective graduate course in rhetorical theory and practice. While all writing instruction at Penn is also coordinated by the English department, it is offered through two separate programs. Unlike many other AAU writing programs, Penn's has no writing requirement: the freshman English seminars are a large part of the Freshman Seminar Program, through which students may satisfy humanities requirements. The second program is an example of the cross-curricular programs developing across the country, though it is in fact younger and less comprehensive than some. This program, Writing across the University (WATU), offers no courses at all but, rather, supplies teaching assistants or consultants to help integrate writing into courses offered by various departments. The Expository Writing Program at Harvard is one of the few AAU programs that are independent. This program offers a required one-semester writing course, taught in six different "sorts," an advanced course, and a recently developed remedial course.

The administrative structures of these three programs suggest the range of alternatives being tried on campuses across the country. Writing programs now fit on a spectrum, many remaining within English departments but some having various degrees of independence. Even those within English departments vary widely in structure, depending on their nature and scope. At North Carolina, Chapel Hill, which as yet has no program for writing across the curriculum, all courses are united under the director and the Freshman Committee. At Penn, each of the two separate programs has its own coordinator, reporting to the chair of the department. Michigan also has two programs, though one exists outside the English department. There, the English Composition Board handles writing assessment and coordinates the sizable cross-curricular program, and the English department's Program in Composition offers freshman and advanced writing instruction. Two administrative units are joined as one at UCLA, where Writing Programs combines a subdepartment of English (the Composition Section) with an independent office assigned to develop new courses and programs campuswide. The writing program at Minnesota, Minneapolis, while independent, is closely related to the English department. The director and faculty are budgeted in the composition program but tenured in English, though they could conceivably hold appointments in other departments. Finally, the independent program at Harvard is related to the English department only through the director, who, though his doctorate is in history, teaches in the English department, where he has recently taken an additional appointment.

These programs represent different structural solutions to the problem of what a writing program should be. Each solution is governed by theoretical assumptions about the "discipline," as well as by the practical realities of campus life. Even decisions made for the most pragmatic reasons reveal and influence attitudes toward composition. For example, the decision to leave a writing program within English or to pull it out might be based on political alliances as much as on conviction. At the same time, the judgment will also suggest how important writing seems and how extensive and well-heeled a writing program should be. On the other end of the scale, a similar decision based on a thoughtful analysis of composition's disciplinary status will also require attention to the practical details of budgets and teaching assignments. Within any of the programs described above, writing could be well taught and the teaching of writing could gain esteem. None therefore seems the best or the only model to be advocated. Together, however, these models suggest the effort and imagination going into program design, and they show the range of options that have been developed. Individually, they represent careful solutions that seem to be working well. On each campus, the choice of administrative structure is extremely important, for it can substantially affect a program's stature and well-being, as well as all its operations.

Structural differences in writing programs—together with variations in resources, needs, and expectations—result in widely differing types of administrative appointments. As we have seen, directors in the programs visited hold quite different positions. At North Carolina, Chapel Hill, Erika Lindemann is an associate professor in the English department. As director of composition, she reports to the chair, and she is advised by a committee of faculty members and teaching assistants who are given responsibility for individual freshman writing courses. At Penn, Peshe Kuriloff and David Espey also hold appointments in English and report to the chair, but they are designated coordinators; Kuriloff is coordinator of Writing across the University and the Writing Center, and Espey is coordinator of freshman English and graduate studies. (In the year following this study, Kuriloff's title was changed to director of University Writing Projects.) Both hold half-time administrative and half-time teaching appointments, renewable annually. At Harvard, Richard Marius is a senior lecturer in expository writing. Though this position is also a half-time administrative and half-time faculty appointment, it continues without limitation of time. And, as Marius explains: " . . . standard practice is for senior lecturers to stay their lives here. Robert Lowell was a senior lecturer" (letter to the author, 20 June 1985). Marius reports to the associate dean for undergraduate studies and serves on the standing committee that makes appointments in the program, on recommendation from the program's hiring committee.

To see these appointments in context, recall some of the figures on directors in AAU writing programs. Of the 42 respondents holding academic appointments, 14 are professors and 17 are associate professors, while 5 are assistant professors, 3 are lecturers or instructors, and 3 hold other titles. (While Marius is one of those holding other academic titles, his title does not indicate an insecure position.) Further, 31 of the 44 respondents are already tenured and another 6 are on the tenure track, leaving only 7 with term appointments. Lindemann's appointment, then, is quite typical of those held by the administrators of AAU writing programs. While Marius's is unusual in its features, it is like many others in its security and stature. Kuriloff and Espey are among the minority here in holding renewable annual appointments. They see some advantages in having administrative rather than faculty positions, however. They do not view their appointments as unstable; in fact, Espey's is not funded on soft money. As Kuriloff explains, "Unlike many writing program administrators, who are also junior faculty, we do not have to concern ourselves with tenure. This [freedom] allows us to operate fairly autonomously and with more hope for the future than many assistant professors experience" (letter to the author, 8 Dec. 1985).

In this set of appointments, we see the director's need for both stability and authority. Tenure and a professorship offer both, but not all universities recognize composition in any form as a legitimate field of scholarly endeavor. Directors who take on composition as a second field may be hard pressed to develop proper credentials, both because they are working in two fields and because work in composition is often questioned during reviews for promotion and tenure. It is still much easier for an established academic to move into this field than for young faculty members working in the field to reach top ranks. As we have seen, this pattern has begun changing at some universities. Until that change becomes more pervasive, however, personnel cases involving writing program directors and faculty members will continue to need great care and attention. One director pointed out that since these are still special cases, they should be prepared for over a period of years: the scholarly domain should be defined and placed in its university context long before a decision on tenure is pending. He feels strongly that those who will influence the decision should understand the original appointment and the specific areas of responsibility assigned. On some campuses, as we have seen, directors hold administrative, rather than faculty, appointments. While some of these may be secure and appropriate, others may simply represent easy solutions to a vexing problem.

Not only the directors' appointments but also those of others teaching writing vary widely in AAU programs. Again, the range can be seen in the case studies. At North Carolina, Chapel Hill, where the program is secured within the English department, writing courses are taught by regular faculty members and teaching assistants. At Penn they are taught almost exclusively by graduate students, appointed as teaching fellows. Most fellows teaching freshman seminars are from the English department, though during 1984-85 some came from American civilization, comparative literature, education, folklore, and the Annenberg School of Communications. Teachers in the WATU program represent many departments in addition to English, such as those named above. Most expository writing courses at Harvard are taught by writers holding annual appointments. Preceptors, who teach full-time, may have their appointments renewed for up to eight years of service. Teaching assistants, who teach part-time, may serve up to four years or, in special cases, six. A few courses are taught by graduate students, appointed as teaching fellows.

Together, the programs on these three campuses suggest the dilemmas of staffing now common to writing programs. If a program is housed in an English department, regular faculty members may not want to teach its courses. If they don't teach in the program, questions can be raised about the department's commitment to teaching writing and about the program's status in the department. But even if regular faculty members do teach writing, some may show less interest or perhaps less expertise in teaching these courses than would the composition specialists or carefully trained teaching assistants who may be competing to teach them. Bringing in temporary faculty members to teach writing involves dangers for those hired and for the program. Even if temporary faculty members are treated as professionals, they cannot gain tenure or the status of those holding tenure. And even if they are highly qualified teachers, they may not become integrated into the academic community. Relying on graduate students for much of this teaching also has drawbacks: they generally begin as novices, they have to balance their teaching and their own graduate studies, and they can enter and leave the program in large numbers.

Although the program directors may not have control over the number and mix of teachers in any of these ranks, they have found various ways of preparing and supporting those who teach in the program while also giving the instructors some degree of responsibility for it. Of the three campuses studied, North Carolina, Chapel Hill, clearly has the greatest ladder-faculty involvement. In addition to teaching writing courses, as all—or nearly all— English faculty members do, some serve each year on the Freshman Committee and several have in fact directed the program. Those on the Freshman Committee work with the graduate-student members to review and modify the course descriptions and syllabi appearing in the staff manual, and they advise new teaching assistants as well.

At Harvard, though no ladder faculty teach in the program, those holding temporary full-time appointments now take some responsibility for it, overseeing individual courses and helping with program evaluation and hiring. While Marius's Informal Notes for Teachers of Expository Writing sets forth the philosophy and practices of his program, his guidelines remain "informal," so that they can change over time, evolving with the program itself. All teachers in the program also participate in staff meetings on a regular basis. In these ways, the preceptors, teaching assistants, and teaching fellows help to shape the program they teach in.

The graduate students who teach in the programs at North Carolina, Chapel Hill, and Penn take part in training programs, described below. At Chapel Hill, some influence the program through their work on the Freshman Committee, and at Penn several experienced writing fellows in WATU are now acting as senior fellows, advising their colleagues and apparently also becoming involved in program development. Through the work of the fellows, WATU provides support for faculty members across campus and raises the level of attention given writing. Some faculty members have also been panelists or speakers in the colloquiums presented by WATU. More extensive programs involving faculty members or preparing them for teaching writing have been designed on some campuses. At Vanderbilt, for example, Scott Colley has conducted workshops for 80 of the 390 faculty members on campus. A number of campuses—including Brown; UCLA; Catholic; Chicago; Michigan; Nebraska, Lincoln; Purdue; and USC—have hosted conferences on writing for local or national audiences.

In the context of the structures, appointments, and practices outlined above, consider the scope of the programs themselves. At North Carolina, Chapel Hill, and at Harvard, freshman writing courses predominate, with some advanced courses available as well. A similar pattern would have held at Penn before the introduction of WATU, which now supports writing instruction in many departments and at many levels. In none of these programs, however, do we see the depth or variety of advanced writing courses we would find, for example, at Maryland, College Park, where the courses are required, or at UCLA, where they are elective. The writing courses at Maryland are taught in four areas: humanities, natural science and technology, social science, and business. Those at UCLA are of several types: advanced courses, with special sections for students interested in such fields as business or law; adjunct courses for students concurrently enrolled in courses in various departments; courses for students earning credentials in education; and courses and internships in practical writing and editing. These advanced courses are elements of writing-across-the-curriculum programs. UCLA's offerings extend from programs for the local schools to graduate writing courses in such fields as history and dentistry. Maryland serves all students in both their freshman and their junior years. These programs, like WATU at Penn, suggest some of the approaches being tried in the 18 AAU writing programs studied that now have responsibility for writing across the curriculum.

At the graduate level, the courses and workshops offered by the programs visited prepare graduate students—in English or other departments—for teaching writing. With 100 graduate students in English teaching writing each year, North Carolina, Chapel Hill, is like other schools in facing the need for a continuing and large-scale TA-training program. Maryland, College Park, for example, normally has 85 TAs in English, and Indiana, Bloomington, has 120. North Carolina's solution, described above, includes orientation and workshops, together with a staff manual and classroom visits, as well as the personal support of the director and a freshman committee. Both Maryland, College Park, and Indiana, Bloomington, add another dimension to training, using mentor systems in which experienced TAs advise novices.

The task is somewhat different at Penn, however. There, since 1981, graduate students in English have been trained primarily through a graduate course, English 800, so that the teacher of the course and the coordinator of freshman English serve as the students' mentors. The relatively new challenge is to prepare graduate students from other departments to work as writing fellows in WATU. This training is now accomplished through a program of orientation, workshops, and colloquiums. A more intensive program has been developed at Chicago for the graduate students from various departments selected for the Advanced Professional Writing program (the Little Red Schoolhouse). They attend a seminar on writing, devoting three weeks to the course itself, four weeks to composition theory, and three weeks to classroom practices. In what may be the country's largest program using graduate students from various fields to teach writing courses, USC—with a staff of 159 teaching in its Freshman Writing Program during 1984-85—offers a two-week summer orientation program, followed by a one-semester staff-development seminar for new instructors. For continuing staff development, every instructor belongs to an instructional coordinating group of 10 to 15 members, meeting twice a month to exchange ideas on teaching writing and to discuss methods of improving instruction.

At some universities, as we have seen, graduate students are not only trained to teach writing as they earn advanced degrees but also prepared for careers in writing, whether in academic or other professions. It is possible for graduate students at Harvard, Penn, and North Carolina, Chapel Hill, to develop concentrations in rhetoric and composition and write dissertations on relevant topics. Other schools have already developed strong doctoral programs to begin preparing the next generation of theorists and practitioners. During 1984-85, 20 of the 65 graduate students in the English department at Pittsburgh were working in composition. Similarly, Purdue, having developed a graduate program in rhetoric and composition in 1981, had 38 MA and PhD students working in the field. Indiana, Bloomington, approved a new PhD program on language, literature, and literacy in 1984-85. Carnegie-Mellon has three undergraduate majors in writing, two MA programs (in professional writing and in literary theory, rhetorical theory, and creative writing), and a PhD in rhetoric. The English department itself has undergone what Gary Waller has described as a double revolution, first in composition and now in literary and cultural studies.

In this context, we can see that the effort to develop sound, effective programs on the campuses I visited parallels a larger effort to give composition focus and coherence as a field of study. While Harvard, Penn, and North Carolina, Chapel Hill, lack forceful graduate programs in rhetoric and composition, they do have ambitious writing programs that work. They are trying to offer the instruction needed on their campuses and to offer it in ways that are philosophically defensible and administratively sound. They are working hard to find and hold their proper places in their own universities.

How much is now required for a writing program to be judged successful? Ironically, the goal of improving the writing of all students on campus—and doing so in all the ways that are both sound and au courant—may be simply beyond reach. Just as it would be unreasonable to assume that any writing program could hire, assign, or influence enough faculty members and offer enough classes to influence all students at all stages of their university careers, so too it is unreasonable to think that everything going on in composition studies and all the alternatives, pedagogical or administrative, being tried on campuses today could or should be integrated into the practices of any one writing program. And who would argue that any program should be expected to do all this? The work being done today, the assumptions being made about what writing programs at their very best might do—these are correctives to the notion that writing is a simple matter, best learned in school and confined at the university to innocuous, quiet classrooms and well-behaved freshman English programs. But what I see happening now is this: to demonstrate the value of our work, some of us directing writing programs, teaching in them, or doing research in the field want very much to announce that we have found not just a better way to proceed, but the right way. The danger is that we will become prescriptive and intolerant, and the study I've done argues, if for anything at all, for tolerance.

The question that must be asked, however, is how the work being done on single campuses bears on that being done elsewhere and how, more generally, developments on any campus advance and help define the "profession" or the "discipline" of composition. There is an outward pressure here, the actions and decisions on individual campuses becoming larger than they are as they become known and as they signal change. Composition is changing, as a subject of teaching and research and as a subject that falls within the province of writing programs, wherever they themselves may lie. For that reason, the attitudes toward composition and the alignments between English departments and writing programs seen in the case studies deserve tracing here. Those attitudes and alignments are neither completely representative nor fully unique: while none of these campuses has gone through what might be described as a revolution in composition, or a double revolution in composition and in literary and cultural studies, together they form one wave of such a revolution, occurring nationally. Though their progress is neither steady nor equal, and though the direction of change is not at all times the same, these programs do show alternative ways of fitting composition into the academy.

At North Carolina, Chapel Hill, while composition is not—at least not yet—viewed as a field of study equal to others, the writing program is solidly lodged within the English department. I say that composition is not equal to, say, medieval literature, because of the evidence in faculty appointments and graduate programs. But Erika Lindemann is indeed encouraged to work in this field, and this professional activity is considered to her credit, both qualifying her for her administrative position and helping her advance in the faculty ranks. It is true, however, that she was familiar to her colleagues when she was hired: she had earned her PhD in the department, specializing in medieval literature. While the chair and other department members also view composition as a legitimate field of endeavor, some question remains about whether a composition specialist could be appointed as an assistant director in the program. Graduate students regard their work in the writing program as integral to their study and preparation for academic careers, though few, or perhaps none, are now specializing in the field.

In spite of these discrepancies, the writing program has a secure position within the department, and its work is seen as important to the university. Though the program has so far remained essentially contained within the department, it now seems to have support and occasion for expansion. Responsibility for teaching writing is already shared, in that a recent campus-wide review gave writing an important place in the curriculum. In the academic year following that of the study, a faculty committee was considering ways of emphasizing writing across the curriculum.

Notice here the different values attaching to the fact of writing's belonging to, inhering within, a "program." On the one hand, a writing program is a familiar thing. This recognition in part surely helps account for its well-being in the department. Its being a limited and defined program and fitting within a similarly clearly circumscribed unit called a department may also partly account for its not having ranged too far beyond that department. Lindemann has worked with high school teachers, and some of them are introduced into the department as students or interns, but no major efforts have yet been made by or for the program to transcend the departmental lines that divide the campus into parts. The support for writing that has been gained has moved through other channels—faculty committees and the administration (in consultation with Lindemann and in support of her program)—but it has not been channeled through the program itself. Writing on this campus has what it often lacks elsewhere and what some other program directors are working hard to get: institutional endorsement. Now institutional endorsement is not the same thing as funding (just as spoken commitments do not always equal performance), but it is a sine qua non for broad and continuing success in the academy.

It does seem now as if the program at Chapel Hill might expand—if not in size, at least in reach. I'm not suggesting that "the program" should take over the effort to help writing infuse the curriculum. Many directors I spoke with emphasized the importance of broad faculty support and of others initiating an effort to move into a new stage of development on campus. But some, Joseph Williams in particular, also made it clear that when this initiative is presented and a need for more concerted action is recognized, the writing program and those in it must be ready to help and to know what to do. Note again the concept of "program": it may not be necessary or wise to bring into the writing program all efforts to improve writing, but the program may help lend coherence to all—or much—that goes on, giving these endeavors a kind of programmatic design. I qualify this statement on design because I don't want to rule out or, by implication, underestimate the significance of what happens spontaneously, without design.

While the English department gives Penn's two writing programs their identity and base, they transcend departmental lines. As part of the Freshman Seminar Program, the freshman English seminars have university-wide status. Though they are elective, they help students satisfy humanities requirements, and most freshmen take them. At the same time as the seminars have this range, however, they are firmly grounded in the subject within the purview of the English department, English and American literature. This freshman program, then, is like and unlike other freshman writing programs: it derives its character from literature and it is housed in the English department, but its courses—"seminars"—are like the seminars offered in other departments, usually by ladder faculty members, often by distinguished professors. One point of difference between English and other seminars, of course, is that the English seminars are now taught by graduate students, though I understand there is some discussion of changing this practice. Nevertheless, these English courses, by analogy with the seminars offered outside the department, take on an aura of importance and dignity that is sometimes, perhaps usually, lacking in freshman English as traditionally construed.

The second program, Writing across the University, indicates by its name that its purpose is campuswide, but again, housed in English, it has the support and the departmental affiliation it needs. From this base, the program can work with graduate and undergraduate students, as well as with faculty members, across campus. This program parallels the freshman English seminars but also diverges from them. While the freshman seminars are part of a band reaching across the university at the freshman level and serving students during their freshman year, WATU is a small program administratively restricted to the English department but aiming to serve students in any department and at any point during their university careers. The freshman program, then, differs structurally from traditional freshman writing programs, and WATU also differs from them conceptually.

The programs' base in English is important: in addition to providing support and protection, the department confers a kind of academic legitimacy. This is not the legitimacy of a full-fledged field of study—except perhaps nominally—for though the department authorized a tenure or tenure-track appointment in composition, it did so in a year of restricted budgeting, and an appointment was made in Renaissance rather than in composition. But the department has aggressively incorporated the work being done in the field, first through hiring Elaine Maimon as a consultant and then through developing a cross-curricular program that reflects some of the best understandings and aims of the most innovative writing programs in the country. Though WATU as yet lacks permanent funding, writing instruction is receiving attention and gaining a place within the English department and across campus. In part, WATU's difficulty with funding suggests not just its newness but also the difficulty of working an innovative campuswide program into the fabric of the institution.

At Harvard, we find yet another conception of "program." The Expository Writing Program is to some extent analogous to the departments of English, French, history, and physics on campus, though it is smaller and more restricted in scope. When we turn from those departments to the writing program, the reduction in scale is obvious: Expository Writing is primarily a freshman program, with some offerings at advanced levels. It does not have a full-scale upper-division course of study; it has no majors. It offers no graduate courses; it has no degree candidates. But it does not depend for its existence on any department; instead, it stands beside them, its director being much like a department chair. Its links to the established disciplines are through the students, who write in courses across campus; through the standing committee, which plays an advisory role; and through the director, who is now beginning to work with the teaching fellows of various departments and to join other faculty members in serving on university committees and performing other university and public functions.

Here, composition is redefined as writing, and writing includes creative writing, even though the program is called Expository Writing. This definition of composition may be richer and deeper than others, though some might argue that it is more limited, failing to draw deeply on the research and theory of the field. Richard Marius, the program's director, points out that he is indeed open to hiring composition specialists, any approved by his hiring committee and the standing committee, and that his staff-training sessions often focus on work in composition; he just doesn't give this kind of work precedence in his program. More important to him are the facts of writing, publishing, talking about writing, and teaching it well. This program is based on experience, the process of writing, more than on the notion of composition as an academic discipline. He argues that composition has learned in the past ten years what writers have always known, that writing is a process: appropriately, that process is itself the foundation of his program, both in the selection of teachers and in their performance in the classroom, the process of writing always being highlighted in their classes and in their remarks on their students' writing.

Marius, himself a writer and a scholar, has proper academic credentials, though not in rhetoric and composition and not in English literature. He is a journalist, a historian, and a novelist. He was appointed not for his work in composition but for his scholarly accomplishments, and he has been allowed to pursue the interests growing out of his work in this program. His relationship with the English department has been positive, and he has recently taken an added appointment in that department. He has for years taught a seminar on teaching expository writing in college, and he can now direct the work of graduate students.

While in none of the case-study programs does composition have the standing of an established scholarly academic discipline, in all of them writing seems academically legitimate. Each is developing a different solution to the problem of authority. At North Carolina, Chapel Hill, the program appears at least loosely analogous to a field of study within English studies and secure within the department. The authority given by this identity is complemented by the authority of tradition, arising within the department certainly, but also more broadly within the university that the program fits so well. At Penn, the authority of both freshman English and WATU seems to be lent primarily by the institution itself. While both gain authority from participating in a larger service than the English department alone would provide, they also derive authority from that department, which gives their endeavors shelter and legitimacy. At Harvard, the Expository Writing Program has the standing given by its administrative likeness to a department. Within the program another type of authority has developed, that of community. Donald Stone stresses the importance of the program's attitude toward itself, and this program clearly sees itself as an academic community, a community of writers.

In composition right now, authority is not something that is bestowed, that comes from outside, from "the profession." Authority does depend on the state of the profession, the stature of those working in the field, and the coherence of the endeavor (established through such means as professional organizations, meetings, journals, and graduate programs). But full authority cannot yet be derived from these sources, and maybe it never should be, given the nature of the enterprise. Now, at least, these elements are not enough. Therefore, success depends also on the individuals teaching in and directing programs; on the relationships and alliances, formal and informal, developed on campuses; on the distributions of power within the university administration and within departments; on resources and support; on the kinds of investigations and experiments being carried out—pedagogical, intellectual, and administrative. Writing is both a profession and a form of intensive labor: it cannot be separated from the practical realities of classrooms and offices, faculty and administrative.

While this discipline is in flux, decisions being made on individual campuses continue to have particular importance. Certainly, the form of inquiry into composition influences the character of writing programs, but the direction of influence can also be reversed: the form and coherence of individual writing programs bear on the nature and status of the discipline itself. Struggling for power and authority, writing programs test the discipline and expose the academic politics and traditions that lead us to expect any legitimate study to become a discipline. Even here, I've come to refer to composition as a discipline, not because I've answered the question of what it is, but because I need a term to describe it. Naturally, language is available not only to describe this reality but to shape it.

This entire work has, finally, been focused on the act of definition. We've seen attempts to define the role and the potential of writing programs within the academy. And we've heard directors explain why they would define composition as a discipline, a field, or an interdisciplinary study. This effort at definition is not yet finished, nor should it be. Programs continue to change and to readjust their fit within their institutions. Efforts to design sound writing programs are not simply directed toward the constituent faculty members and students; these efforts also affect departments across campus and, increasingly, campuses across the country. Questions about the disciplinary status of composition lead to questions about normal academic structures and traditions. Overall, writing programs that have long existed somewhere on the periphery seem now to be redefining the center and the periphery. This endeavor is both a linguistic and an administrative exercise, one that can only strengthen the writing programs and the academy.

Influential Texts

C URIOUSLY, COMPOSITION HAS SO FAR produced very little discourse on its own discourse. The field is indeed receiving much attention in print: Is composition a discipline? What are the characteristics of composition as a discipline or field of study? Who are the figures shaping it? What kind of research is appropriate and needed? How are composition and English studies related, intellectually and administratively? How should writing programs be managed and writing courses taught? These questions show an important self-consciousness about what composition is and what it might become. But this field of language study has not yet scrutinized its own language or texts.

With composition only now evolving, or reclaiming its former identity and status, many of its key questions are being addressed in journal articles or collections of essays. Its basic works include bibliographical essays, points of departure for research, sourcebooks for teachers, and textbooks or style manuals. When the field is viewed as "rhetoric and composition" or just "rhetoric," a full set of works on the history, theory, and practice of rhetoric is added to the shelves. And when it is viewed as an interdisciplinary study, or at least an interdisciplinary practice (writing being used in every discipline), it acquires works produced in other fields (psychology, philosophy, or education, for example).

Works Named by Program Directors

Because I was curious to know what books influence those now directing writing programs, I added this item to my survey: "Please cite six books (in any field) that you consider important to your work as a writing program administrator." I expected the responses to do three things: (1) suggest some works considered central to the study, teaching, and practice of writing; (2) show something about the backgrounds and interests of those directing writing programs; and (3) possibly turn up some works relevant to managing these—or other—academic programs. The results, though unscientific, satisfied my curiosity.

Most respondents listed works in composition or rhetoric: the books named most often are by Shaughnessy, Moffett, Tate and Corbett (together and individually), Kinneavy, Lindemann, and Elbow. Britton should be included here, though the citations were divided between two books, lowering the tallies for each. Next come works by Berthoff, Horner, Strunk and White, and Witte and Faigley. Books cited twice are by a wide range of authors, including not only Beach and Bridwell, Christensen, Cooper and Odell but also Booth, Hirsch, Williams, Bruner, Dewey, and Piaget. Textbooks appear in this portion of the list (Corbett, Maimon), as do style manuals (Strunk and White, Zinsser). Both practice and theory are represented (Tate and Corbett, Lindemann; Kinneavy, Burke).

Single entries on the list show works in composition, rhetoric, literary theory, philosophy, psychology, the history of science, and—how shall I classify *Zen and the Art of Motorcycle Maintenance*? Perhaps that book should be the first entry under management (or academic administration), which includes as well works by Drucker, Ebel, and Keller. Finally, several business, education, and composition journals were mentioned—among them, *WPA* (the journal of the Council of Writing Program Administrators). And two dictionaries were named (*OED* and *Webster's Second*).

Notes written in response to this question addressed the problems of administration: "No book is important: many years of experience in teaching, editing, and writing are what counts." "Books don't really help me with angry students, plagiarism cases, upset graduate fellows, or budget wheedling." "There just aren't any books that help with administration." Nine people did not respond to the question. In a cover letter (18 Jan. 1985), Richard Marius offered this explanation:

> Everything I learned about administration came from my father, who for many years managed a foundry in Lenoir City, Tennessee, that manufactured all the freight car wheels for Southern Railway. He walked through the place every day and spoke to everybody he saw. He had four hundred people working for him. He treated them with great respect and listened to them and sometimes fired them with compassion. (One man he fired came in and announced that he would have to kill my father in response; my father, not a large man, threw him through the glass door to the office but then refused to press charges against him.) Anyway, that is all I know about this job, and it seems almost surprising to me that there are so few helpful books. I suppose the WPA journal may be a contribution here.

Using short titles and few middle initials, I offer the complete list of works named, along with the number of times each was mentioned:

Nine Mentions

Shaughnessy, Mina. *Errors and Expectations.*

Six Mentions

Moffett, James. *Teaching the Universe of Discourse.*
Tate, Gary, ed. *Teaching Composition: 10 Bibliographical Essays.*
Tate, Gary, and Edward P. J. Corbett. *The Writing Teacher's Sourcebook.*

Five Mentions

Corbett, Edward P. J. *Classical Rhetoric for the Modern Student.*
Kinneavy, James. *A Theory of Discourse.*
Lindemann, Erika. *A Rhetoric for Writing Teachers.*

Four Mentions

Elbow, Peter. *Writing without Teachers.*

Three Mentions

Berthoff, Ann. *The Making of Meaning.*
Britton, James. *Language and Learning.*
Britton, James, et al. *The Development of Writing Abilities (11-18).*
Horner, Winifred, ed. *Literature and Composition: Bridging the Gap.*
Strunk, William, Jr., and E. B. White. *The Elements of Style.*
Witte, Stephen, and Lester Faigley. *Evaluating College Writing Programs.*

Two Mentions

Beach, Richard, and Lillian Bridwell, eds. *New Directions in Composition Research.*
Booth, Wayne. *Modern Dogma and the Rhetoric of Assent.*
Bruner, Jerome. *Toward a Theory of Instruction.*
Burke, Kenneth. *A Grammar of Motives.*
Christensen, Francis. *Notes toward a New Rhetoric.*
Cooper, Charles, and Lee Odell. *Research on Composing.*
Dewey, John. *Experience and Education.*
Hirsch, E. D., Jr. *The Philosophy of Composition.*
Irmscher, William. *Teaching Expository Writing.*
Macrorie, Kenneth. *Telling Writing.*
Maimon, Elaine, et al. *Writing in the Arts and Sciences.*
Murray, Donald. *A Writer Teaches Writing.*
Piaget, Jean. (No title indicated.)
Williams, Joseph. *Style: Ten Lessons in Clarity and Grace.*
Zinsser, William. *On Writing Well.*

One Mention

Aristotle. *Rhetoric.*
Arthur, Bradford. *Teaching English to Speakers of English.*
Brandt, W., et al. *The Craft of Writing.*

Coles, William, Jr. *The Plural I.*
Crane, Ronald. *The Languages of Criticism and the Structure of Poetry.*
Donovan, Timothy, and Ben McClelland, eds. *Eight Approaches to Teaching Composition.*
Dowling, William. *The Critic's Hornbook.*
Drucker, Peter. *Management.*
Eble, Kenneth. *The Art of Administration.*
Frederiksen, Carl, and Joseph Dominic, eds. *Writing.* Vol. 2.
Freud, Sigmund. *Introductory Lectures on Psychoanalysis.*
Glaser, Robert. *Advances in Instructional Psychology.*
Graves, Richard, ed. *Rhetoric and Composition.*
Hammond, Eugene. *Teaching Writing.*
Keller, George. *Academic Strategy.*
Kuhn, Thomas. *The Structure of Scientific Revolutions.*
Langer, Susanne. *Philosophy in a New Key.*
Lanham, Richard. *Literacy and the Survival of Humanism.*
———. *Style: An Anti-Textbook.*
———. (No title indicated.)
Mathes, J. C., and Dwight Stevenson. *Designing Technical Reports.*
Meiland, Jack. *College Thinking.*
Murphy, James, ed. *The Rhetorical Tradition and Modern Writing.*
Neman, Beth. *Teaching Students to Write.*
Nystrand, Martin. *What Writers Know.*
Perelman, Chaim. *The New Rhetoric.*
Pirsig, Robert. *Zen and the Art of Motorcycle Maintenance.*
Plato. *The Gorgias; The Phaedrus.*
Quirk, Randolph, and Sidney Greenbaum. *A Concise Grammar of Contemporary English.*
Raymond, James, ed. *Literacy as a Human Problem.*
Robinson, W. S. "The Written English Sentence" (unpublished).
Rosenblatt, Louise. (No title indicated.)
Sale, Roger. *On Writing.*
Smith, Frank. *Understanding Reading.*
———. Works. (No titles indicated.)
Tibbetts, A. M. *Working Papers.*
Vygotsky, Lev. (No title indicated.)
Walvoord, Barbara. *Helping Students Write Well.*
Whitehead, Alfred North. *The Aims of Education.*
Whiteman, Marcia Farr, ed. *Writing.* Vol. 1.
Wilcox, Thomas. *The Anatomy of College English.*
Zinsser, William. *Writing with a Word Processor.*

In addition, these journals, dictionaries, and other types of material were listed:

Studies in Writing and Rhetoric (Southern Illinois UP)
Chronicle of Higher Education
Harvard Business Review
Harvard Review on Human Relations
NCTE Policy and Position Statements

OED
Webster's Second
WPA: Writing Program Administration

In response to my request to list six influential books, one director replied, "Couldn't even choose six: hundreds of books have been important to my work." Taking my cue from him, I offer a selected bibliography of (more than six) books (and some articles) that have influenced my own work as a writing program director.

A Selected Bibliography

This bibliography is divided into eight sections. The opening three list works on the history and nature of composition, first in relation to English studies and rhetoric, then as a discipline. The entries in the next three deal with the theory and practice of composition. Included here are works on composition theory and its sources; curriculum, pedagogy, and research; and writing across the curriculum. Writing across the curriculum is a separate subdivision because it is important not only pedagogically but also administratively. The effort to improve writing in all disciplines has administrative implications, requiring new classes and structures to carry on this kind of work. The next section concerns a topic not developed in the text but too important to leave out—literacy and the schools. Though my survey didn't focus on work in this area, I include references here to give access to material on the subject. The final section lists works on program administration.

This bibliography should be seen as a work in progress: more citations could be added, and many works could be reclassified. Some entries under "Composition and Rhetoric" would fit as well under "Composition and English Studies." And some works that belong naturally under "Curriculum, Pedagogy, and Research" appear under "Composition as a Discipline" instead because they have helped to give this field identity and direction. I've placed them here only to suggest that such works can be formative while a field is developing rapidly. Other books and articles could have been handled similarly. As I worked on this bibliography, the number of entries grew and the classifications became increasingly more difficult to hold. I considered using a single alphabetical listing, but I did want, with broad strokes, to divide these works into categories relevant to this study.

1. Composition and English Studies

Applebee, Arthur N. *Tradition and Reform in the Teaching of English: A History.* Urbana: NCTE, 1974.
Booth, Wayne C. "The Common Aims That Divide Us: Or, Is There a 'Profession 1981'?" *Profession 81.* New York: MLA, 1981. 13-17.

Cowan, Elizabeth Wooten, ser. ed. *Options for the Teaching of English: The Undergraduate Curriculum*. New York: MLA, 1975.

Demetz, Peter, et al. "Report of the Commission on the Future of the Profession, Spring 1982." *PMLA* 97 (1982): 940-58.

Douglas, Wallace. "Rhetoric for the Meritocracy: The Creation of Composition at Harvard." *English in America: A Radical View of the Profession*. By Richard Ohmann with a chapter by Wallace Douglas. New York: Oxford UP, 1976. 97-132.

Gerber, John C. "A Glimpse of English as a Profession." *Profession 77*. New York: MLA, 1977. 26-33.

———. "Suggestions for a Commonsense Reform of the English Curriculum." *College Composition and Communication* 28 (1977): 312-16. Rpt. in *The Writing Teacher's Sourcebook*. Ed. Gary Tate and Edward P. J. Corbett. New York: Oxford UP, 1981. 20-26.

Hairston, Maxine. "Breaking Our Bonds and Reaffirming Our Connections." *ADE Bulletin* 81 (1985): 1-5. Rpt. in *College Composition and Communication* 36 (1985): 272-82.

Halloran, S. Michael. "What Every Department Chair Should Know about Scholarship in Technical Communication." *ADE Bulletin* 79 (1984): 43-45.

Hillocks, George, Jr., ed. *The English Curriculum under Fire: What Are the Real Basics?* Urbana: NCTE, 1982.

Hirsch, E. D., Jr. "Remarks on Composition to the Yale English Department." *The Rhetorical Tradition and Modern Writing*. Ed. James J. Murphy. New York: MLA, 1982. 13-18.

Hollingsworth, Alan M. "Beyond Survival." *Profession 77*. New York: MLA, 1977. 7-11.

Horner, Winifred Bryan, ed. *Composition and Literature: Bridging the Gap*. Chicago: U of Chicago P, 1983.

Hunter, J. Paul. "Facing the Eighties." *Profession 80*. New York: MLA, 1980. 1-9.

Johnson, Paula. "Writing Programs and the English Department." *Profession 80*. New York: MLA, 1980. 10-16.

Kitzhaber, Albert R. "Rhetoric in American Colleges, 1850-1900." Diss. U of Washington, 1953.

———. *Themes, Theories, and Therapy: The Teaching of Writing in College*. New York: McGraw, 1963.

Lanham, Richard A. "Composition, Literature, and the Lower-Division Gyroscope." *Profession 84*. New York: MLA, 1984. 10-15.

Lloyd-Jones, Richard. "Writing Programs and the English Department." *ADE Bulletin* 61 (1979): 17-22.

Marius, Richard. "The Precarious Opportunity: The University Writing Program." *National Forum* 65.4 (1985): 16-20.

Miller, James E., Jr. "ADE and the English Coalition." *ADE Bulletin* 81 (1985): 16-19.

Miller, Susan. "What Does It Mean to Be Able to Write? The Question of Writing in the Discourses of Literature and Composition." *College English* 45 (1983): 219-35.

Moglen, Helene. "Erosion in the Humanities: Blowing the Dust from Our Eyes." *Profession 83*. New York: MLA, 1983. 1-6.

Neel, Jasper P., ed. *The State of the Discipline, 1970s-1980s*. Spec. issue of *ADE Bulletin* 62 (1979).

Ohmann, Richard. *English in America: A Radical View of the Profession*. New York: Oxford UP, 1976.

Parker, William Riley. "Where Do English Departments Come From?" *College*

English 28 (1967): 339-51. Rpt. in *The Writing Teacher's Sourcebook*. Ed. Gary Tate and Edward P. J. Corbett. New York: Oxford UP, 1981. 3-19.

Peterson, Linda. "Getting a Little Help from Our (Literary) Friends." *WPA* 5.3 (1982): 15-20.

Robinson, Jay L. "Literacy in the Department of English." *College English* 47 (1985): 482-98.

Schaefer, William D. "Curiouser and Curiouser." *Profession 81*. New York: MLA, 1981. 18-24.

———. "Still Crazy after All These Years." *Profession 78*. New York: MLA, 1978. 1-8.

Scholes, Robert. *Textual Power: Literary Theory and the Teaching of English*. New Haven: Yale UP, 1985.

Schulz, Max, and Michael Holzman. "English Departments—Writing Programs: Marriage or Divorce?" *ADE Bulletin* 70 (1981): 26-29.

Smith, Paul. "The Tests and the Discipline." *Profession 78*. New York: MLA, 1978. 28-31.

Steinmann, Martin, Jr. "What's the Real Crisis?" *Profession 78*. New York: MLA, 1978. 9-12.

Stewart, Donald C. "Some Facts Worth Knowing about the Origins of Freshman Composition." *CEA Critic* 44.4 (1982): 2-11.

———. "Two Model Teachers and the Harvardization of English Departments." *The Rhetorical Tradition and Modern Writing*. Ed. James J. Murphy. New York: MLA, 1982. 118-29.

Vendler, Helen. "Presidential Address 1980." *PMLA* 96 (1981): 344-50.

Waller, Gary F. "Working within the Paradigm Shift: Poststructuralism and the College Curriculum." *ADE Bulletin* 81 (1985): 6-12.

Watt, Ian. "On Not Attempting to Be a Piano." *Profession 78*. New York: MLA, 1978. 13-15.

White, Edward M. "Post-structural Criticism and the Response to Student Writing." *College Composition and Communication* 35 (1984): 186-95.

Widdowson, Peter, ed. *Re-reading English*. New Accents. London: Methuen, 1982.

Wilcox, Thomas W. *The Anatomy of College English*. San Francisco: Jossey, 1973.

Young, Art, Mike Gorman, and Margaret Gorman. "The 1983-84 Writing and Literature Survey: Courses and Programs." *ADE Bulletin* 79 (1984): 48-55.

2. Composition and Rhetoric

Berlin, James A. "Rhetoric and Poetics in the English Department: Our Nineteenth-Century Inheritance." *College English* 47 (1985): 521-33.

Booth, Wayne C. "The Scope of Rhetoric Today: A Polemical Excursion." *The Prospect of Rhetoric*. Ed. Lloyd F. Bitzer and Edwin Black. Report of the National Developmental Project, Sponsored by the Speech Communication Association. Englewood Cliffs: Prentice, 1971. 93-114.

Connors, Robert J. "Mechanical Correctness as a Focus in Composition Instruction." *College Composition and Communication* 36 (1985): 61-72.

———. "The Rhetoric of Explanation: Explanatory Rhetoric from Aristotle to 1850." *Written Communication* 1 (1984): 189-210.

———. "The Rhetoric of Explanation: Explanatory Rhetoric from 1850 to the Present." *Written Communication* 2 (1985): 49-72.

Connors, Robert J., Lisa S. Ede, and Andrea A. Lunsford. *Essays on Classical Rhetoric and Modern Discourse*. Carbondale: Southern Illinois UP, 1984.

Corbett, Edward P. J. *Classical Rhetoric for the Modern Student*. 2nd ed. New York: Oxford UP, 1971.

Corder, Jim W. "On the Way, Perhaps, to a New Rhetoric, but Not There Yet, and if We Do Get There, There Won't Be There Anymore." *College English* 47 (1985): 162-70.

————. "Rhetoric and Literary Study: Some Lines of Inquiry." *College Composition and Communication* 32 (1981): 13-20.

————. "Studying Rhetoric and Teaching School." *Rhetoric Review* 1 (1982): 4-36.

D'Angelo, Frank J. *A Conceptual Theory of Rhetoric*. Cambridge: Winthrop, 1975. 1975.

Freedman, Aviva, and Ian Pringle, eds. *Reinventing the Rhetorical Tradition*. Published for the Canadian Council of Teachers of English. Conway: L & S, U of Central Arkansas, 1980.

Horner, Winifred Bryan, ed. *The Present State of Scholarship in Historical and Contemporary Rhetoric*. Columbia: U of Missouri P, 1983.

Kaufer, David S., and Christine M. Neuwirth. "Integrating Formal Logic and the New Rhetoric: A Four-Stage Heuristic." *College English* 45 (1983): 380-89.

Kinneavy, James L. "Restoring the Humanities: The Return of Rhetoric from Exile." *The Rhetorical Tradition and Modern Writing*. Ed. James J. Murphy. New York: MLA, 1982. 19-28.

Lauer, Janice M. "Doctoral Programs in Rhetoric." *Rhetoric Society Quarterly* 10 (1980): 190-94.

Murphy, James J. "Rhetorical History as a Guide to the Salvation of American Reading and Writing: A Plea for Curricular Courage." *The Rhetorical Tradition and Modern Writing*. New York: MLA, 1982. 3-12.

————, ed. *A Synoptic History of Classical Rhetoric*. 1972. Davis: Hermagoras, 1983.

Perelman, Chaim. *The New Rhetoric and the Humanities: Essays on Rhetoric and Its Applications*. Introd. Harold Zyskind. Dordrecht, Hol.: Reidel, 1979.

Raymond, James C. "Rhetoric: The Methodology of the Humanities." *College English* 44 (1982): 778-83.

Stewart, Donald C. "The Status of Composition and Rhetoric in American Colleges, 1880-1902: An MLA Perspective." *College English* 47 (1985): 734-46.

Walter, Otis M. "Plato's Idea of Rhetoric for Contemporary Students: Theory and Composition Assignments." *College Composition and Communication* 35 (1984): 20-30.

Weaver, Richard M. *The Ethics of Rhetoric*. 1953. Davis: Hermagoras, 1985.

Winterowd, W. Ross. *Composition/Rhetoric: A Synthesis*. Carbondale: Southern Illinois UP, 1986.

————. *Contemporary Rhetoric: A Conceptual Background with Readings*. New York: Harcourt, 1975.

————. "The Politics of Meaning: Scientism, Literarism, and the New Humanism." *Written Communication* 2 (1985): 269-91.

3. *Composition as a Discipline*

Braddock, Richard, Richard Lloyd-Jones, and Lowell Schoer, eds. *Research in Written Composition*. Champaign: NCTE, 1963.

Brereton, John, ed. *Traditions of Inquiry*. New York: Oxford UP, 1985.

Burhans, Clinton S., Jr. "The Teaching of Writing and the Knowledge Gap." *College English* 45 (1983): 639-56.

Connors, Robert J. "Composition Studies and Science." *College English* 45 (1983): 1-20.

———. "Journals in Composition Studies." *College English* 46 (1984): 348-65.

Cooper, Charles R., and Lee Odell, eds. *Research on Composing: Points of Departure*. Urbana: NCTE, 1978.

Corder, Jim W. "Outhouses, Weather Changes, and the Return to Basics in English Education." *College English* 38 (1977): 474-82.

D'Angelo, Frank. "Regaining Our Composure." *College Composition and Communication* 31 (1980): 420-26.

de Beaugrande, Robert. "Linguistic Theory and Composition." *College Composition and Communication* 29 (1978): 134-40.

———. "Psychology and Composition." *College Composition and Communication* 30 (1979): 50-57.

Eckhardt, Caroline D., and David H. Stewart. "Towards a Functional Taxonomy of Composition." *College Composition and Communication* 30 (1979): 338-42.

Fulkerson, Richard. "Four Philosophies of Composition." *College Composition and Communication* 30 (1979): 343-48.

Gage, John T. "Freshman English: In Whose Service?" *College English* 44 (1982): 469-74.

Gorrell, Robert M. "Like a Crab Backward: Has the CCCC Been Worth It?" *College Composition and Communication* 30 (1979): 32-36.

Graves, Richard L. "Renaissance and Reform in the Composition Curriculum." *Phi Delta Kappan* 62 (1981): 417-20.

Lauer, Janice M. "Composition Studies: Dappled Discipline." *Rhetoric Review* 3 (1984): 20-29.

Lloyd-Jones, Richard. "Focus and Resolution." *ADE Bulletin* 57 (1978): 8-12. Rpt. in *The Writing Teacher's Sourcebook*. Ed. Gary Tate and Edward P. J. Corbett. New York: Oxford UP, 1981. 27-35.

———. "What We May Become." *College Composition and Communication* 33 (1982): 202-07.

McQuade, Donald, ed. *The Territory of Language: Linguistics, Stylistics, and the Teaching of Composition*. 1979. Rev. and enlarged. Carbondale: Southern Illinois UP, 1986.

Odell, Lee. "Teachers of Composition and Needed Research in Discourse Theory." *College Composition and Communication* 30 (1979): 39-45.

Phelps, Louise Wetherbee. "Foundations for a Modern Psychology of Composition." *Rhetoric Review* 3 (1984): 30-37.

Pichaske, David R. "Freshman Comp: What Is This Shit?" *College English* 38 (1976): 117-24.

Shaughnessy, Mina P. *Errors and Expectations: A Guide for the Teacher of Basic Writing*. New York: Oxford UP, 1977.

Sommers, Nancy I. "The Need for Theory in Composition Research." *College Composition and Communication* 30 (1979): 46-49.

Stewart, Donald C. "Some History Lessons for Composition Teachers." *Rhetoric Review* 3 (1985): 134-43.

Tate, Gary, ed. *Teaching Composition: 10 Bibliographical Essays*. Fort Worth: Texas Christian UP, 1976.

Troyka, Lynn Quitman. "The Pulse of the Profession." *College Composition and Communication* 31 (1980): 227-31.

4. Composition Theory and Its Sources

Berthoff, Ann E. *Reclaiming the Imagination: Philosophical Perspectives for Writers and Teachers of Writing*. Upper Montclair: Boynton, 1984.

Bizzell, Patricia. "William Perry and Liberal Education. *College English* 46 (1984): 447-54.

Booth, Wayne C. *Modern Dogma and the Rhetoric of Assent*. Chicago: U of Chicago P, 1972.

Britton, James. *Language and Learning*. 1970. Harmondsworth, Eng.: Penguin, 1972.

Bruffee, Kenneth A. "Liberal Education and the Social Justification of Belief." *Liberal Education* 68 (1982): 95-114.

———. "Liberal Education, Scholarly Community, and the Authority of Knowledge." *Liberal Education* 71 (1985): 231-39.

———. "The Structure of Knowledge and the Future of Liberal Education." *Liberal Education* [67] (1981): 177-86.

Bruner, Jerome S. *Toward a Theory of Instruction*. Cambridge: Belknap-Harvard UP, 1966.

Burke, Kenneth. *A Grammar of Motives*. Berkeley: U of California P, 1969.

———. "Questions and Answers about the Pentad." *College Composition and Communication* 29 (1978): 330-35.

Comprone, Joseph. "Kenneth Burke and the Teaching of Writing." *College Composition and Communication* 29 (1978): 336-40.

de Beaugrande, Robert. "Writer, Reader, Critic: Comparing Critical Theories as Discourse." *College English* 46 (1984): 533-60.

Fish, Stanley. *Is There a Text in This Class? The Authority of Interpretive Communities*. Cambridge: Harvard UP, 1980.

Flower, Linda, and John R. Hayes. "A Cognitive Process Theory of Writing." *College Composition and Communication* 32 (1981): 365-87.

Fulkerson, Richard P. "Kinneavy on Referential and Persuasive Discourse: A Critique." *College Composition and Communication* 35 (1984): 43-56.

Hairston, Maxine. "The Winds of Change: Thomas Kuhn and the Revolution in the Teaching of Writing." *College Composition and Communication* 33 (1982): 76-88. Rpt. in *Rhetoric and Composition: A Sourcebook for Teachers*. Ed. Richard L. Graves. New ed. Upper Montclair: Boynton, 1984. 14-26.

Hays, Janice N., Phyllis A. Roth, Jon R. Ramsey, and Robert D. Foulke, eds. *The Writer's Mind: Writing as a Mode of Thinking*. Urbana: NCTE, 1983.

Kinneavy, James L. *A Theory of Discourse: The Aims of Discourse*. Englewood Cliffs: Prentice, 1971.

Kuhn, Thomas S. *The Stucture of Scientific Revolutions*. 2nd ed. Foundations of the Unity of Science. International Encyclopedia of Unified Science 2.2. Chicago: U of Chicago P, 1970.

Langer, Susanne K. *Philosophy in a New Key: A Study in the Symbolism of Reason, Rite, and Art*. 1942. New York: Mentor, 1951.

———. *Problems of Art: Ten Philosophical Lectures*. New York: Scribner's, 1957.

Lanham, Richard A. *Style: An Anti-Textbook*. New Haven: Yale UP, 1974.

Lewis, Clayton W. "Burke's Act in *A Rhetoric of Motives*." *College English* 46 (1984): 368-76.

Moffett, James. *Teaching the Universe of Discourse*. 1968. Upper Montclair: Boynton, 1983.

Ong, Walter J. *Orality and Literacy: The Technologizing of the Word*. New Accents. London: Methuen, 1982.

Perry, William G., Jr. *Forms of Intellectual and Ethical Development in the College Years*. New York: Holt, 1970.

Piaget, Jean. *Science of Education and the Psychology of the Child*. Trans. Derek Coltman. New York: Penguin, 1977.

Polanyi, Michael. *Knowing and Being: Essays by Michael Polanyi*. Ed. Marjorie Grene. Chicago: U of Chicago P, 1969.

——. *Personal Knowledge: Towards a Post-critical Philosophy*. Chicago: U of Chicago P, 1958.

Rorty, Richard. *Philosophy and the Mirror of Nature*. 1979. 2nd prtg. with corrections. Princeton: Princeton UP, 1980.

Scholes, Robert. "Is There a Fish in This Text?" *College English* 46 (1984): 653-64.

Vygotsky, L. S. *Thought and Language*. Ed. and trans. Eugenia Hanfmann and Gertrude Vakar. Cambridge: MIT P, 1962.

Young, Richard E., Alton L. Becker, and Kenneth L. Pike. *Rhetoric: Discovery and Change*. New York: Harcourt, 1970.

5. Curriculum, Pedagogy, and Research

Bartholomae, David. "The Study of Error." *College English* 31 (1980): 253-69. Rpt. in Graves 311-27.

Beach, Richard, and Lillian S. Bridwell, eds. *New Directions in Composition Research*. Foreword by Linda S. Flower and John R. Hayes. New York: Guilford, 1984.

Bereiter, Carl, and Marlene Scardemalia. "Learning about Writing from Reading." *Written Communication* 1 (1984): 163-88.

Berthoff, Ann E. "Is Teaching Still Possible? Writing, Meaning, and Higher Order Reasoning." *College English* 46 (1984): 743-55.

Blount, Nathan S. "Bibliography of Research in the Teaching of English." *Research in the Teaching of English* 1-6 (Spring and Fall issues 1967-72).

Carpenter, Carol. "Exercises to Combat Sexist Reading and Writing." *College English* 43 (1981): 293-300.

Charney, Davida. "The Validity of Using Holistic Scoring to Evaluate Writing: A Critical Overview." *Research in the Teaching of English* 18 (1984): 65-81.

Christensen, Francis, and Bonniejean Christensen. *Notes toward a New Rhetoric: Nine Essays for Teachers*. 2nd ed. New York: Harper, 1978.

Coles, William E., Jr. *The Plural I: The Teaching of Writing*. New York: Holt, 1978.

Collins, James L., and Elizabeth A. Sommers, eds. *Writing On-Line: Using Computers in the Teaching of Writing*. Upper Montclair: Boynton, 1985.

Comprone, Joseph J. "Recent Research in Reading and Its Implications for the College Composition Curriculum." *Rhetoric Review* 1 (1983): 122-38.

Connors, Robert J. "The Rise and Fall of the Modes of Discourse." *College Composition and Communication* 32 (1981): 444-55.

Cooper, Charles R., and Lee Odell, eds. *Evaluating Writing: Describing, Measuring, Judging*. Urbana: NCTE, 1977.

Daiute, Colette. "The Computer as Stylus and Audience." *College Composition and Communication* 35 (1984): 134-45.

Diederich, Paul B. *Measuring Growth in English*. Urbana: NCTE, 1974.

Dietrich, Daniel J. "Annotated Bibliography of Research in the Teaching of English." *Research in the Teaching of English* 7-13 (Spring and Winter issues 1973-77, May and Dec. 1978, May 1979).

Dietrich, Daniel J., and Richard H. Behm. "Annotated Bibliography of Research in the Teaching of English." *Research in the Teaching of English* 13-17 (Dec. 1979, May and Dec. issues 1980-83).

———. "Annotated Bibliography of Research in the Teaching of Literature and the Teaching of Writing." *Research in the Teaching of English* 18 (May 1984).

Donovan, Timothy R., and Ben W. McClelland, eds. *Eight Approaches to Teaching Composition.* Urbana: NCTE, 1980.

Durst, Russel K., and James D. Marshall. "Annotated Bibliography of Research in the Teaching of English." *Research in the Teaching of English* 18-19 (Dec. issues 1984-85).

Elbow, Peter. *Writing without Teachers.* London: Oxford UP, 1973.

———. *Writing with Power: Techniques for Mastering the Writing Process.* New York: Oxford UP, 1981.

Emig, Janet. *The Composing Processes of Twelfth Graders.* Research Report 13. Urbana: NCTE, 1971.

———. *The Web of Meaning: Essays on Writing, Teaching, Learning, and Thinking.* Ed. Dixie Goswami and Maureen Butler. Upper Montclair: Boynton, 1983.

———. "Writing as a Mode of Learning." *College Composition and Communication* 28 (1977): 122-28.

Faigley, Lester, and Thomas P. Miller. "What We Learn from Writing on the Job." *College English* 44 (1982): 557-69.

Flower, Linda, and John R. Hayes. "The Cognition of Discovery: Defining a Rhetorical Problem." *College Composition and Communication* 31 (1980): 21-32.

———. "Problem-Solving Strategies and the Writing Process." *College English* 39 (1977): 449-61. Rpt. in Graves 269-82.

Flower, Linda, et al. "Detection, Diagnosis, and the Strategies of Revision." *College Composition and Communication* 37 (1986): 16-55.

Frederiksen, Carl H., and Joseph F. Dominic. *Writing: Process, Development and Communication.* Hillsdale: Erlbaum, 1981. Vol. 2 of *Writing: The Nature, Development, and Teaching of Written Communication.* 2 vols.

Gebhardt, Richard C. "Changing and Editing: Moving Current Theory on Revision into the Classroom." *Rhetoric Review* 2 (1984): 78-91.

———, ed. *Composition and Its Teaching: Articles from* College Composition and Communication *during the Editorship of Edward P. J. Corbett.* Findlay: Ohio Council of Teachers of English Language Arts, 1979.

Gere, Anne Ruggles. "Empirical Research in Composition." *Perspectives on Research and Scholarship in Composition.* Ed. Ben W. McClelland and Timothy R. Donovan. New York: MLA, 1985. 110-24.

Gere, Anne Ruggles, and Eugene Smith. *Attitudes, Language, and Change.* Urbana: NCTE, 1979.

Gorrell, Robert M. "How to Make Mulligan Stew: Process and Product Again." *College Composition and Communication* 34 (1983): 272-77.

Goswami, Dixie. "Teachers as Researchers." Graves 347-58.

Graves, Richard L., ed. *Rhetoric and Composition: A Sourcebook for Teachers and Writers.* New ed. Upper Montclair: Boynton, 1984.

Hairston, Maxine. "Working with Advanced Writers." *College Composition and Communication* 35 (1984): 196-208.

Halliday, M. A. K., and Ruqaiya Hasan. *Cohesion in English.* English Language Series 9. London: Longman, 1976.

Halpern, Jeanne W., and Sarah Liggett. *Computers & Composing: How the New Technologies Are Changing Writing.* Foreword by Edward P. J. Corbett. Published for the Conference on College Composition and Communication. Carbondale: Southern Illinois UP, 1984.

Hartwell, Patrick. "Grammar, Grammars, and the Teaching of Grammar." *College English* 47 (1985): 105-27.

Irmscher, William F. *Teaching Expository Writing.* New York: Holt, 1979.

Klaus, Carl H., and Nancy Jones, eds. *Courses for Change in Writing: A Selection from the NEH/Iowa Institute.* Upper Montclair: Boynton, 1984.

Kneupper, Charles W. "Teaching Argument: An Introduction to the Toulmin Model." *College Composition and Communication* 29 (1978): 237-41.

Kolln, Martha. "Closing the Books on Alchemy." *College Composition and Communication* 32 (1981): 139-51. Rpt. in Graves 292-304.

Krashen, Stephen D. *Writing: Research, Theory, and Applications.* New York: Pergamon, 1984.

Lanham, Richard A. *Revising Prose.* New York: Scribner's, 1979.

Larson, Richard L. "Selected Bibliography of Research and Writing about the Teaching of Composition." *College Composition and Communication* 26-30 (May issues 1975-79).

Lindemann, Erika. *A Rhetoric for Writing Teachers.* New York: Oxford UP, 1982.

Lunsford, Andrea. "Cognitive Development and the Basic Writer." *College English* 41 (1979): 38-46.

Macrorie, Ken. *Telling Writing.* 3rd ed. Rochelle Park: Hayden, 1980.

———. *Uptaught.* Rochelle Park: Hayden, 1970.

Marshall, James D., and Russel K. Durst. "Annotated Bibliography of Research in the Teaching of English." *Research in the Teaching of English* 19 (May 1985).

Mellon, John C. *Transformational Sentence-Combining: A Method for Enhancing the Development of Syntactic Fluency in English Composition.* 1967. Research Report 10. Champaign: NCTE, 1969.

Meyer, Bonnie J. F. "Reading Research and the Composition Teacher: The Importance of Plans." *College Composition and Communication* 33 (1982): 37-49.

Moran, Michael G., and Ronald F. Lunsford, eds. *Research in Composition and Rhetoric: A Bibliographic Sourcebook.* Westport: Greenwood, 1984.

Murray, Donald M. *Learning by Teaching: Selected Articles on Writing and Teaching.* Upper Montclair: Boynton, 1982.

———. *A Writer Teaches Writing: A Practical Method of Teaching Composition.* 2nd ed. Boston: Houghton, 1984.

Nystrand, Martin, ed. *What Writers Know: The Language, Process, and Structure of Written Discourse.* New York: Academic-Harcourt, 1982.

Odell, Lee, and Dixie Goswami, eds. *Writing in Nonacademic Settings.* New York: Guilford, 1986.

O'Hare, Frank. *Sentence-Combining: Improving Student Writing without Formal Grammar Instruction.* Research Report 15. Urbana: NCTE, 1973.

Perkins, Kyle. "On the Use of Composition Scoring Techniques, Objective Measures, and Objective Tests to Evaluate ESL Writing Ability." *TESOL Quarterly* 17 (1983): 651-71.

Perl, Sondra. "Understanding Composing." *College Composition and Communication* 31 (1980): 363-69. Rpt. in Graves 304-10.

Ponsot, Marie, and Rosemary Deen. *Beat Not the Poor Desk: Writing: What to Teach, How to Teach It, and Why.* Upper Montclair: Boynton, 1982.

Purves, Alan. "In Search of an Internationally-Valid Scheme for Scoring Compositions." *College Composition and Communication* 35 (1984): 426-38.

Rose, Mike. "The Language of Exclusion: Writing Instruction at the University." *College English* 47 (1985): 341-59.

———. "Remedial Writing Courses: A Critique and a Proposal." *College English* 45 (1983): 109-28.

———. "Speculations on Process Knowledge and the Textbook's Static Page." *College Composition and Communication* 34 (1983): 208-13.

———. *Writer's Block: The Cognitive Dimension*. Studies in Writing and Rhetoric. Carbondale: Southern Illinois UP, 1984.

Rouse, John. "An Erotics of Teaching." *College English* 45 (1983): 535-48.

Ruth, Leo, and Sandra Murphy. "Designing Topics for Writing Assessment: Problems of Meaning." *College Composition and Communication* 35 (1984): 410-22.

Schwartz, Helen, and Lillian S. Bridwell. "A Selected Bibliography on Computers in Composition." *College Composition and Communication* 35 (1984): 71-77.

Scott, Patrick, and Bruce Castner. "Reference Sources for Composition Research: A Practical Survey." *College English* 45 (1983): 756-68.

Smith, Frank. *Understanding Reading: A Psycholinguistic Analysis of Reading and Learning to Read*. 3rd ed. New York: Holt, 1982.

Smith, Louise Z. "Composing Composition Courses." *College English* 46 (1984): 460-69.

Sommers, Nancy. "Responding to Student Writing." *College Composition and Communication* 33 (1982): 148-56.

———. "Revision Strategies of Student Writers and Experienced Adult Writers." *College Composition and Communication* 31 (1980): 378-88. Rpt. in Graves 328-37.

Stiggins, Richard. "A Comparison of Direct and Indirect Writing Assessment Methods." *Research in the Teaching of English* 16 (1982): 101-14.

Stock, Patricia L., ed. *fforum: Essays on Theory and Practice in the Teaching of Writing*. Upper Montclair: Boynton, 1983.

Stull, William L. *Combining and Creating: Sentence Combining and Generative Rhetoric*. New York: Holt, 1983.

Tate, Gary, and Edward P. J. Corbett, eds. *The Writing Teacher's Sourcebook*. New York: Oxford UP, 1981.

Tebeaux, Elizabeth. "Redesigning Professional Writing Courses to Meet the Communication Needs of Writers in Business and Industry." *College Composition and Communication* 36 (1985): 419-28.

Toulmin, Stephen. *The Uses of Argument*. Cambridge: Cambridge UP, 1958.

Trimble, John R. *Writing with Style: Conversations on the Art of Writing*. Englewood Cliffs: Prentice, 1975.

Warnock, John. "The Writing Process." *Rhetoric Review* 2 (1983): 4-27.

Williams, Joseph. "The Phenomenology of Error." *College Composition and Communication* 32 (1981): 152-68.

———. *Style: Ten Lessons in Clarity and Grace*. Glenview: Scott, 1981.

Wresch, William, ed. *The Computer in Composition Instruction: A Writer's Tool*. Urbana: NCTE, 1984.

Zinsser, William. *Writing with a Word Processor*. New York: Harper, 1983.

6. *Writing across the Curriculum*

Connelly, Peter J., and Donald C. Irving. "Composition in the Liberal Arts: A Shared Responsibility." *College English* 37 (1976): 668-70.

Cullen, Robert J. "Writing across the Curriculum: Adjunct Courses." *ADE Bulletin* 80 (1985): 15-17.

Forman, Janis. "Notes toward Writing across the Curriculum: Some Collaborative Efforts." *Journal of Basic Writing* 2.4 (1980): 12-21.

Freisinger, Randall R. "Cross-Disciplinary Writing Workshops: Theory and Practice." *College English* 42 (1980): 154-66.

Fulwiler, Toby. "How Well Does Writing across the Curriculum Work?" *College English* 46 (1984): 113-25.

———. "Showing, Not Telling, at a Writing Workshop." *College English* 43 (1981): 55-63. Rpt. in *Rhetoric and Composition: A Sourcebook for Teachers and Writers.* New ed. Ed. Richard L. Graves. Upper Montclair: Boynton, 1984. 338-46.

Fulwiler, Toby, and Art Young, eds. *Language Connections: Writing and Reading across the Curriculum.* Urbana: NCTE, 1982.

Griffin, C. W. "Programs for Writing across the Curriculum: A Report." *College Composition and Communication* 36 (1985): 398-403.

———. ed. *Teaching Writing in All Disciplines.* New Directions for Teaching and Learning 12. San Francisco: Jossey, 1982.

Hamilton, David. "Interdisciplinary Writing." *College English* 41 (1980): 780-96.

Hartwell, Patrick, and Greg Waters. "Reinventing the Rhetorical Tradition: Finding Ways to Revalue Writing." *Forum for Liberal Education* 7 (1984): 2-4.

Herrington, Anne J. "Classrooms as Forums for Reasoning and Writing." *College Composition and Communication* 36 (1985): 404-13.

———. "Writing to Learn: Writing across the Disciplines." *College English* 43 (1981): 379-87.

Kinneavy, James L. "Writing across the Curriculum." *Profession 83.* New York: MLA, 1983. 13-20.

Knoblauch, C. H., and Lil Brannon. "Writing as Learning through the Curriculum." *College English* 45 (1983): 465-74.

Maimon, Elaine P. "Cinderella to Hercules: Demythologizing Writing across the Curriculum." *Journal of Basic Writing* 2.4 (1980): 3-11.

———. "Comprehensive Writing Programs: Keeping Them Going." *Forum for Liberal Education* 7 (1984): 4-5.

———. "Writing in the Arts and Sciences: Getting Started and Gaining Momentum." *WPA* 4.3 (1981): 9-13.

Moffett, James. *Active Voice: A Writing Program across the Curriculum.* Upper Montclair: Boynton, 1981.

Press, Harriet Baylor. "Basic Motivation for Basic Skills: The Interdependent Approach to Interdisciplinary Writing." *College English* 41 (1979): 310-13.

Raimes, Ann. "Writing and Learning across the Curriculum: The Experience of a Faculty Seminar." *College English* 41 (1980): 797-801.

Siegel, Muffy E. A., and Toby Olson, eds. *Writing Talks: Views on Teaching Writing from across the Professions.* Upper Montclair: Boynton, 1983.

Smith, Barbara Leigh. "An Interview with Elaine Maimon." *Current Issues in Higher Education* 3 (1983-84): 11-15.

———. "Writing across the Curriculum: What's at Stake?" *Current Issues in Higher Education* 3 (1983-84): 1-3.

Weiss, Robert, and Michael Peich. "Faculty Attitude Change in a Cross-Disciplinary Writing Workshop," *College Composition and Communication* 31 (1980): 33-41.

7. Literacy and the Schools

Applebee, Arthur N., with Anne Auten and Fran Lehr. *Writing in the Secondary School: English and the Content Areas.* Foreword by Charles Cooper. Research Report 21. Urbana: NCTE, 1981.

Bailey, Richard W., and Robin Melanie Fosheim, eds. *Literacy for Life: The Demand for Reading and Writing.* New York: MLA, 1983.

Boyer, Ernest L. *High School: A Report on Secondary Education in America.* Carnegie Foundation for the Advancement of Teaching. New York: Harper, 1983.

Commission on the Humanities. *The Humanities in American Life: Report of the Commission on the Humanities*. Berkeley: U of California P, 1980.

Cooper, Charles R., ed. *The Nature and Measurement of Competency in English*. Urbana: NCTE, 1981.

Coughlin, Ellen K. "Literacy: 'Excitement' of New Field Attracts Scholars of Literature." *Chronicle of Higher Education* 9 Jan. 1985: 1, 10.

Glatthorn, Allan A. *A Guide for Developing an English Curriculum for the Eighties*. Urbana: NCTE, 1980.

Grant, Steven A. "Language Policy in the United States." *Profession 78*. New York: MLA, 1978. 32-42.

Holzman, Michael. "The Social Context of Literacy Education." Opinion. *College English* 48 (1986): 27-33.

Johnson, Paula. "The Politics of 'Back to Basics.'" *Profession 77*. New York: MLA, 1977. 18-21.

Lanham, Richard A. *Literacy and the Survival of Humanism*. New Haven: Yale UP, 1983.

Lyons, Gene. "The Higher Illiteracy: On the Prejudice against Teaching College Students to Write." *Harper's* Sept. 1976: 33-40.

McPherson, Elisabeth. "The Significance of the Written Word." *Profession 77* (1977): 22-25.

Myers, Miles. "Shifting Standards of Literacy—The Teacher's Catch-22." *English Journal* 4 (1984): 26-32.

National Commission on Excellence in Education. *A Nation at Risk: The Imperative for Education Reform*. Washington: GPO, 1983.

Olson, Lynn. "Let Them Write: The Call for More Time on Task." *Education Week* 5 Sept. 1984: L12, L50.

Ong, Walter J. "Literacy and Orality in Our Time." *ADE Bulletin* 58 (1978): 1-7. Rpt. in *The Writing Teacher's Sourcebook*. Ed. Gary Tate and Edward P. J. Corbett. New York: Oxford UP, 1981. 36-48.

Pattison, Robert. *On Literacy: The Politics of the Word from Homer to the Age of Rock*. New York: Oxford UP, 1982.

Raymond, James C., ed. *Literacy as a Human Problem*. University: U of Alabama P, 1982.

Stubbs, Michael. *Language and Literacy: The Sociolinguistics of Reading and Writing*. London: Routledge, 1980.

Tanner, James E. "The Ethics of Literacy Training." *College English* 44 (1982): 18-24.

Troyka, Lynn Quitman. "Perspectives on Legacies and Literacy in the 1980s." *College Composition and Communication* 33 (1982): 252-62.

Whiteman, Marcia Farr, ed. *Variation in Writing: Functional and Linguistic-Cultural Differences*. Hillsdale: Erlbaum, 1981. Vol. 1 of *Writing: The Nature, Development, and Teaching of Written Communication*. 2 vols.

Williams, Joseph M. "Who's Responsible for Whose Language?" *Profession 77*. New York: MLA, 1977. 12-17.

8. *Program Administration*

Booth, Wayne C. "A Cheap, Efficient, Challenging, Sure-Fire and Obvious Device for Combatting the Major Scandal in Higher Education Today." *WPA* 5.1 (1981): 35-39.

CCCC Committee on Teaching and Its Evaluation in Composition. "Evaluating Instruction in Writing: Approaches and Instruments." *College Composition and Communication* 33 (1982): 213-29.

CCCC Task Force on the Preparation of Teachers of Writing. "Position Statement on the Preparation and Professional Development of Teachers of Writing." *College Composition and Communication* 33 (1982): 446-49.

Connolly, Paul, and Teresa Vilardi, eds. *New Methods in College Writing Programs: Theories in Practice.* New York: MLA, 1986.

Davis, Barbara Gross, Michael Scriven, and Susan Thomas. *The Evaluation of Composition Instruction.* Inverness: Edgepress, 1981.

Furcron, Margaret. "The *WPA* Guide to Planning and Organizing Regional Academic Conferences." *WPA* 4.3 (1981): 23-51.

Gordon, Joseph W., and Linda H. Peterson. "Writing at Yale: Past and Present." *ADE Bulletin* 71 (1982): 10-14.

Gracie, William J., Jr. "Directing Freshman English: The Role of Administration in Freshman English Programs." *WPA* 5.3 (1982): 21-24.

Hairston, Maxine. "We're Hiring Too Many Temporary Instructors." Point of View. *Chronicle of Higher Education* 17 Apr. 1985: 80.

Hammond, Eugene. "Freshman Composition—Junior Composition: Does Coordination Mean Sub-ordination?" *College Composition and Communication* 35 (1984): 217-21.

Haring-Smith, Tori, et al. *A Guide to Writing Programs: Writing Centers, Peer Tutoring Programs, and Writing-across-the-Curriculum.* Glenview: Scott, 1985.

Hartzog, Carol P. "Freshman English 1984: Politics and Administrative Process." *WPA* 8.1-2 (1984): 7-15.

Heller, Scott. "50 Lecturers Lose Their Jobs in a Dispute over How—and If—Writing Can Be Taught." *Chronicle of Higher Education* 17 Apr. 1985: 23-24.

————."3 Tales of Life off the Tenure Track." *Chronicle of Higher Education* 17 Apr. 1985: 23, 25.

Holzman, Michael. "Articulating Composition." *College English* 45 (1983): 288-95.

Lederman, Marie Jean, Michael Ribaudo, and Susan Remmer Ryzewic. "A National Survey on the Assessment and Improvement of the Academic Skills of Entering Freshmen: Some Implications for Writing Program Administrators." *WPA* 7.3 (1984): 11-16.

Lindemann, Erika. "Evaluating Writing Programs: What an Outside Evaluator Looks For." *WPA* 3.1 (1979): 17-24.

Matalene, Carolyn B. "Objective Testing: Politics, Problems, Possibilities." *College English* 44 (1982): 368-81.

McClelland, Ben W. "Part-Time Faculty in English Composition: A WPA Survey." *WPA* 5.1 (1981): 13-20.

McQuade, Donald A. "The Case of the Migrant Workers." *WPA* 5.1 (1981): 29-34.

Nash, George. "Who's Minding Freshman English at U. T. Austin?" *College English* 38 (1976): 125-31.

Neel, Jasper P., ed. *Options for the Teaching of English: Freshman Composition.* New York: MLA, 1978.

Olson, Gary A., ed. *Writing Centers: Theory and Administration.* Urbana: NCTE, 1984.

Potts, Maureen, and David Schwalm. "A Training Program for Teaching Assistants in Freshman English." *WPA* 7.1-2 (1983): 47-54.

Siegel, Gerald, ed. *The CEA Directory of Writing Programs in the United States and Canada.* College Station: CEA, 1980.

Trillin, Alice Stewart, et al. *Teaching Basic Skills in College.* Jossey-Bass Series in Higher Education. San Francisco: Jossey, 1980.

Wallace, M. Elizabeth. "The Richness of Language and the Poverty of Part-Timers: Impact and Invisibility." *College English* 46 (1984): 580-86.

Weinman, Geoffrey S. "A Part-Time Freshman Writing Staff: Problems and Solutions." *WPA* 5.1 (1981): 21-28.

White, Edward M. *Teaching and Assessing Writing.* San Francisco: Jossey, 1985. 1985.

Winterowd, W. Ross. "Developing a Composition Program." *Reinventing the Rhetorical Tradition.* Ed. Aviva Freedman and Ian Pringle. Published for the Canadian Council of Teachers of English. Conway: L & S, U of Central Arkansas, 1980. 157-71.

Witte, Stephen P., Paul R. Meyer, Thomas P. Miller, and Lester Faigley. "A National Survey of College and University Writing Program Directors." Bound printout. Writing Program Assessment Project Technical Report 2. U of Texas, Austin, 31 Aug. 1981.

Works Cited

Applebee, Arthur N. *Tradition and Reform in the Teaching of English: A History.* Urbana: NCTE, 1974.

Cowan, Elizabeth Wooten, ser. ed. *Options for the Teaching of English: The Undergraduate Curriculum.* New York: MLA, 1975.

Cullen, Robert J. "Writing across the Curriculum: Adjunct Courses." *ADE Bulletin* 80 (1985): 15-17.

Fish, Stanley. *Is There a Text in This Class? The Authority of Interpretive Communities.* Cambridge: Harvard UP, 1980.

Gere, Anne Ruggles. "Empirical Research in Composition." *Perspectives on Research and Scholarship in Composition.* Ed. Ben W. McClelland and Timothy R. Donovan. New York: MLA, 1985. 110-24.

Hairston, Maxine. "We're Hiring Too Many Temporary Instructors." Point of View. *Chronicle of Higher Education* 17 Apr. 1985: 80.

Heller, Scott. "50 Lecturers Lose Their Jobs in a Dispute over How—and If—Writing Can Be Taught." *Chronicle of Higher Education* 17 Apr. 1985: 23-24.

———. "3 Tales of Life off the Tenure Track." *Chronicle of Higher Education* 17 Apr. 1985: 23, 25.

Horner, Winifred Bryan, ed. *Composition and Literature: Bridging the Gap.* Chicago: U of Chicago P, 1983.

Kinneavy, James L. "Writing across the Curriculum." *Profession 83.* New York: MLA, 1983. 13-20.

Kitzhaber, Albert R. "Rhetoric in American Colleges, 1850-1900." Diss. U of Washington, 1953.

———. *Themes, Theories, and Therapy: The Teaching of Writing in College.* New York: McGraw-Hill, 1963.

Lauer, Janice M. "Composition Studies: Dappled Discipline." *Rhetoric Review* 3 (1984): 20-29.

Morris, Barbra S. "The English Composition Board at the University of Michigan." *Literacy for Life: The Demand for Reading and Writing.* Ed. Richard W. Bailey and Robin Melanie Fosheim. New York: MLA, 1983.

Murphy, James J. "Rhetorical History as a Guide to the Salvation of American Reading and Writing: A Plea for Curricular Courage." Murphy, *Rhetorical Tradition* 3-12.

———, ed. *The Rhetorical Tradition and Modern Writing.* New York: MLA, 1982.

Neel, Jasper P., ed. *Options for the Teaching of English: Freshman Composition.* New York: MLA, 1978.

Olson, Gary A., ed. *Writing Centers: Theory and Administration*. Urbana: NCTE, 1984.

Parker, William Riley. "Where Do English Departments Come From?" *The Writing Teacher's Sourcebook*. Ed. Gary Tate and Edward P. J. Corbett. New York: Oxford: 1981. 3-19.

Scholes, Robert. *Textual Power: Literary Theory and the Teaching of English*. New Haven: Yale UP, 1985.

Stewart, Donald C. "Two Model Teachers and the Harvardization of English Departments." Murphy, *Rhetorical Tradition* 118-29.

Witte, Stephen P., Paul R. Meyer, Thomas P. Miller, and Lester Faigley. "A National Survey of College and University Writing Program Directors." Bound printout. Writing Program Assessment Project Technical Report 2. U of Texas, Austin, 31 Aug. 1981.